Mastering Math Facts
Addition & Subtraction

Richard Piccirilli

NEW YORK • TORONTO • LONDON • AUCKLAND • SYDNEY
MEXICO CITY • NEW DELHI • HONG KONG • BUENOS AIRES

Teaching
Resources

This work is dedicated to Fraye, who puts up with me daily. Thanks for being patient.

Acknowledgments

No book is written without help from others. First and foremost, I thank my assistant, Todd A. Zuk, without whom this book could not be written. Others who have helped inspire and shape my work include my elementary, undergraduate, and graduate students. Their needs and questions have encouraged me to pursue ideas that support math learning across the grade levels. And to my parents for helping make me who I am.

Content editing by Nicole Iorio
Editorial assistance by Elizabeth Tredeau
Cover design by Brian LaRossa
Interior design by Melinda Belter
ISBN-13: 978-0-545-06405-7
ISBN-10: 0-545-06405-8

Contents

INTRODUCTION

This is a book of practical ideas. It differs from other books that deal with number facts in that it offers a systematic and flexible approach to teaching the 100 addition and subtraction facts. The approach ensures that students retain math facts.

The current focus on problem solving in elementary mathematics often leaves little time for formal instruction in number facts. Not surprisingly, reduced time for number-fact instruction corresponds with a decline in students' computation proficiency—a critical building block for mathematics work, including problem solving. Using *Mastering Math Facts: Addition and Subtraction* helps you ensure that your students all master their math facts and build a solid foundation for growth in mathematics.

Following the *Mastering Math Facts* approach, you'll help students learn basic addition and subtraction facts with efficiency, ease, and confidence. To lead students toward mastery, you'll identify every student's areas of strength and need in a simple manner, which will assist your planning. Then you'll use the strategy tips and suggestions throughout the book to avoid common pitfalls that prevent students from grasping number facts. An important premise of this book is that the time students spend working on addition facts leads naturally to the mastery of subtraction facts. Once they've mastered addition facts, they'll find subtraction facts quick and easy.

How This Book Is Organized

There are two main sections in this book. The first focuses on addition and the second on subtraction. Five chapters make up each section. At the start of each section, you'll find background information that will help you teach the five sequential steps in learning number facts, focused first on addition and then transitioning to subtraction.

In the beginning of the book, you'll find ideas on informal assessment, both for the class and for individual students. The next step is planning. You'll find suggestions for teaching the nature of number facts, followed by one on knowing what pitfalls to avoid. You'll learn about timed tests, as well as how to help students prepare for them through practice and drill.

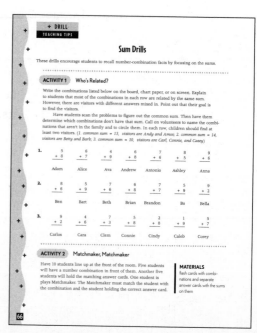

- ## Where do I start?

You choose where it's best for you to begin. A natural place to start is with informal whole-group assessment. For addition facts, you might start with the teacher-led whole-group activities such as the Sum Drills on page 66. You may also begin with small-group games that serve as informal assessment, which you can find on page 74. Start with pages 128 and 129, for subtraction facts, as well as flash-card activities, such as What's the Hidden Number? (page 131). These activities give you insight about the needs of your class.

Flexibility is key. Once you understand the five steps to mastery, you'll want to start where students need support. There are numerous activities and reproducibles from which you can choose.

Suggestions for Planning Number-Fact Lessons

• The Nature of Number-Fact Learning

Emphasize with students that addition is an easier way of counting, and that subtraction undoes addition. By providing experiences with these principles, students will realize the value of addition and subtraction facts, as well as the relationship between the two.

There are one hundred number combinations for addition and for subtraction. These come from all the one-digit number combinations for addition and their subtraction inverses. You'll be working with numbers 0–9. Combinations grouped with their answers are what we'll call "number facts."

Number-fact learning can be accomplished with five sequential steps. Teaching the steps in order gives students a strong foundation and a path to mastery. Keep in mind that not all students will be on the same step at the same time. Once individual needs are identified, group students with similar needs and start with the step most appropriate for each group.

The Five-Step Sequence to Mastery

1. Teach the meaning of number facts.
As the first step, students need to understand the process of adding and subtracting. They need to know what the processes do as they define each skill.

2. Teach strategies.
Strategies make number-fact learning less stressful and easier to learn. Using patterns, students reduce their workload and learning time—a big motivator to master their facts!

3. Provide practice.
Students need to engage in practice that reinforces strategies and broadens the meaning of the process. Practice helps students see relationships among the facts.

4. Provide meaningful drill.
Meaningful drill aids students in knowing number facts at an automatic level. This kind of drill should be given only after students are comfortable with the first three steps.

5. Assess and reteach.
Assessing students is key to helping them identify their strengths and weaknesses. The results of this diagnostic approach give you and your students clear direction for what remedial work may be needed.

Pitfalls to Avoid

By understanding why many students do not know their number facts, you can plan preventative measures. Some of the pitfalls that affect students include:

1. Students do not understand what number facts mean and how the facts help them in math.

2. Students feel overwhelmed when they see all one hundred addition and subtraction facts that need to be learned. They treat each number fact in isolation and do not see patterns and relationships among the facts as an aid.

3. Students count on their fingers, use tally marks, make drawings, or use some other crutch. They are comfortable with this method and do not appreciate the greater efficiency of knowing their addition and subtraction facts.

4. Students have no systematic way to identify what facts they know and don't know. Students may continue to study facts they already know and do not focus on the ones that they do not know because the facts have not been clearly identified for them.

5. Students don't know what to do when they don't know certain number facts. They don't have alternative ways to figure out answers to basic facts.

6. Students have no useful strategies to cut down the workload. They don't have simple names for strategies and don't put into practice what they intuitively know.

7. Teachers don't teach sequential steps to mastery. Students often do not have the background to do the drill and assessment that are asked of them.

8. Learning facts is not viewed by students as fun. Teachers lead practice and drills that are not interactive, enjoyable, or based on previous learning.

THE TRUTH ABOUT TIMED TESTS

Timed tests are an integral part of mastering basic number facts.

1. Timed tests should generally start at Grade 2.

2. Timed tests are drills designed to take what is known and make it automatic.

3. Expect that students work at a reasonable speed, allowing for individual student needs. A baseline measure is for students to recall a fact within 2 to 3 seconds.

4. Premature drill and lack of readiness interfere with the effectiveness of timed tests.

5. Number facts need to be automatic because basic number facts are the foundation for problem solving and higher-order thinking skills. They are prerequisites to most math concepts. Quick mental computations are part of number literacy.

Building Success: A Summary of Suggestions

The following suggestions summarize important elements in this book and include additional daily instruction tips. You likely know many intuitively, but they are worthwhile reminders.

1. Devote class time to number-fact learning. It shows students that you value the benefits of addition- and subtraction-fact mastery.

2. Discuss strategies daily. Help students appreciate how helpful strategies can be. Make strategies part of your math talk. Classroom posters, charts, and class-made videos can explain strategies and highlight their value.

3. Make number facts fun. Both you and your students should enjoy number-fact instruction. Use games frequently. Lead class discussions, solve story problems, use the computer, make illustrations, and do hands-on activities. Have students work in teams and in pairs to make mastery of number facts collaborative.

4. Confer with students regularly. Meet with children who are having trouble remembering facts. Assess their difficulty and strategize how to help. Support students in class and solicit support at home by providing flash cards and other materials.

5. Monitor progress as a motivational technique. Make students' achievement visible. Have students record the results of their quizzes and practice tests so that they feel vested in their learning. Meet with students informally to give them feedback and encouragement as they set and reach goals.

6. Recognize and reward achievement growth. As often as you can, write comments on student papers and send notes home to announce successes. Recognize students through certificates of achievement, badges, and student-of-the-day honors. Communicate with parents on report cards and at parent-teacher conferences.

7. Review number facts often. Short and frequent sessions, which last only a few minutes, can be effective in helping students develop a quick recall of facts.

8. Empower students. If students don't know an answer, support and remind them of strategies they've learned. Students shouldn't feel helpless when they don't know a number fact.

9. Develop positive attitudes. Help students avoid common pitfalls. Help children see that practice, drill, and practice tests are intended to build their confidence as they strive to achieve. Use timed tests wisely to build success. (See Chapters 4, 5, 9, and 10.)

10. Set high expectations. Expect results from students and communicate that you are confident that all students are capable of achieving mastery. Some students may need special attention in order to transition from using crutches such as finger counting or tally marks to memorizing facts. Support them as they improve.

Chapter 1

MAKING MEANING

STEP 1   Teach the Meaning of Addition Facts

In order to master number facts, students need basic knowledge of numbers, counting, and number operations. Children know how to count and are comfortable with counting. Your job is to stress that using number facts to do addition will help them work faster and have more fun. Students will find that once they master number facts for addition, they'll have an easier time finding a total than by counting.

To make learning meaningful, use concrete materials for children to explore. With manipulatives, students improve at counting and learn number patterns. They also begin making associations and seeing relationships. They will learn to compose numbers and decompose numbers. They learn, too, about how numbers act when you put things together. In short, students will develop an intuition about numbers, or number sense.

The goal of this chapter is to teach students to

- Count by patterns
- Use addition as an easier way of counting
- Add by counting-on
- Add-on to 5 and 10

- ## What's in this chapter?

The chapter begins with problem solving using manipulatives, which gives a context for counting and prepares students for counting by patterns. Next, recognizing patterns is introduced. You'll find activities that encourage children to use patterns and faster ways of counting that lead into addition.

The chapter culminates with additional experiences for students to do addition using patterns and the adding-on concept. Your teaching will emphasize adding-on while using the numbers 5 and 10 as anchors.

Early Addition

As they work through problems, students learn to recognize the role of counting in finding totals. Have students solve the story problems below, using a combination of techniques. Show pictures, offer counters, try role playing, and model setting up number sentences to solve the problems. Encourage discussion, and challenge children by asking them to justify answers. These problems are just a start. Make up story problems of your own and encourage students to generate their own, as well. Provide opportunities for students to exchange story problems to solve.

ACTIVITY   Using Counting to Represent Numbers in Everyday Problems

1. At the soccer game, Lucia scored 2 goals and her twin brother, Luca, scored 1 goal. How many goals did the twins score?

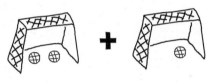

2 + 1 = 3 goals

2. The vet told Deanne to give her growing puppy, Charlie, 3 bones during the day and 2 more at night. How many bones should Deanne feed her dog?

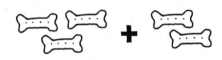

3 + 2 = 5 bones

3. Ken chose 5 girls from his class to be on his team. Next, he chose 4 boys from the class next door. How many other children did Ken pick for his team?

5 + 4 = 9 children

4. Ben's grandmother made spaghetti and meatballs. The meatballs were so good that Ben ate 3 and his mom ate 2. How many meatballs were eaten?

3 + 2 = 5 meatballs

5. While at the airport, Olivia watched 6 airplanes take off. Just 5 minutes later, she saw 4 more planes take off. How many planes did Olivia see take off?

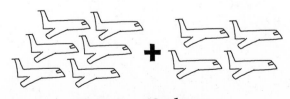

6 + 4 = 10 planes

6. Neeraj has 7 new school pencils. His brother, Neeral, has the same number of pencils. How many pencils do they have all together?

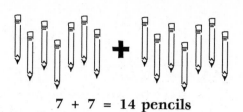

7 + 7 = 14 pencils

7. Fraye likes to play Mother, May I? On her first turn, Fraye took 7 giant steps. On her second turn Fraye took 4 giant steps. How many giant steps did Fraye take in all?

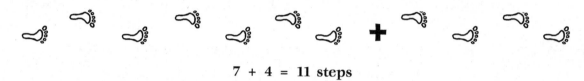

7 + 4 = 11 steps

8. While on the school playground, Latoya counted 8 maple trees and 6 oak trees. How many trees did Latoya count?

8 + 6 = 14 trees

CHALLENGE PROBLEMS

There were 5 horses in the field, and 4 had riders. How many did not have riders?

5 riders = 4 + 1

Bella had 10 cents. Now she has 7 cents. How many pennies did Bella spend?

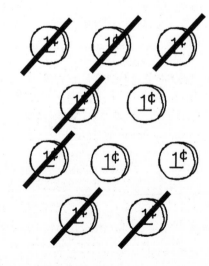

10 pennies = 7 + 3

Counting by Patterns

To practice add-on counting, students need to first recognize the pattern and then count or add-on to the pattern. Make four sets of patterns cards for your class, as seen below. Pages 12–13 include activities you can use with these cards.

Directions for Making Pattern Cards

1. Choose 5- by 8-inch or 3- by 5-inch index cards. Or, cut tagboard.

2. Make circles on each card to form patterns. Suggestions for making circles: trace coins, use self-adhesive dots, or glue objects such as colored discs, beans, or buttons.

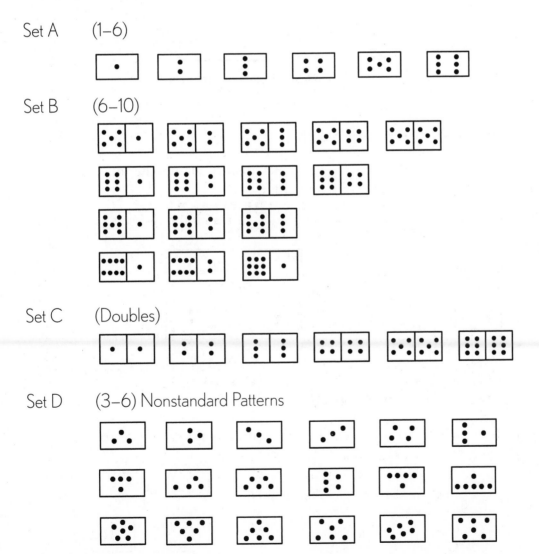

Set A   (1–6)

Set B   (6–10)

Set C   (Doubles)

Set D   (3–6) Nonstandard Patterns

Counting by Patterns

These activities are to be used with the pattern cards described on page 11. Many of the activities can be used with one or more sets of pattern cards. Choose which set or sets of cards best suit the activity you want to use. Be sure to review the cards with children before they begin the following activities.

MATERIALS
Pattern cards (directions: page 11), chart paper/scrap paper for scoring, bulletin-board materials

---

ACTIVITY 1 Patterns from Memory

After students look at a pattern for a few seconds, remove the pattern. Have them use counters to count out the number of objects in the pattern. They can also duplicate the pattern itself by focusing on positions of the dots.

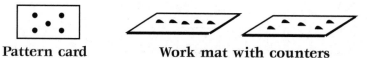

Pattern card   **Work mat with counters**

ACTIVITY 2 Pattern-Number Quick Match

Show a set of pattern cards in order, and have students identify the number of dots without counting. Repeat. This time, put cards in random order.

Variation: Make a duplicate set of cards and have students match the two sets.

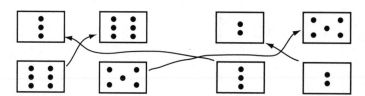

ACTIVITY 3 Scoring Totals With Pattern Cards

Make a pile of pattern cards, facedown. Have two or more students select a card. Ask each child to identify the total number of dots on the card. A point is awarded to the player with the higher number. Repeat until one player scores ten points. He or she is the winner.

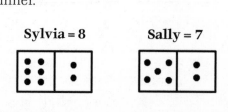

Sylvia = 8   **Sally = 7**

ACTIVITY 4   Scoring Totals With Pattern Cards

Mix all of the sets of cards. Have students separate them into two piles by feature. For example, one pile may have cards with fewer than five dots and the other with more than five dots.

Less than 5 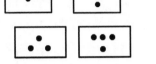   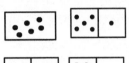 **More than 5**

ACTIVITY 5   Matching Equivalent Patterns

Using **Set B** (6–10) only, have students match the cards that have the same total number of dots.

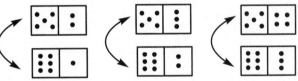

ACTIVITY 6   Recognizing Patterns in Nonstandard Positions

To recognize patterns and totals in nonstandard positions, use **Set B** pattern cards and turn the cards so that each one is positioned to show the smaller number of dots on the left side. Ask: *How many dots are on each card?*

ACTIVITY 7   Interactive Pattern Card Bulletin Board

Use the pattern cards to create a bulletin-board display. Arrange the cards randomly. Point to the cards and have children identify the number of dots.

Variation 1: One student points and the other students respond.

Variation 2: One student points to a pattern card and two students respond. The first to answer correctly earns a point.

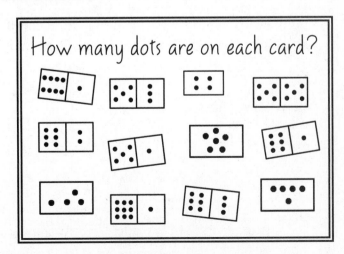

How many dots are on each card?

Addition by Counting-on

Students will improve their addition skills by practicing problems in which they add-on and count-on, beginning with numbers other than one. These suggestions use different kinds of materials for tactile learning.

MATERIALS
Overhead projector or interactive whiteboard, counters, deck of playing cards, cup, chart paper

ACTIVITY 1 Counting-on On screen

On screen, display three counters. Ask: *How many are there?* Count. *How many will there be if one more is added?* Add another counter and count, this time beginning with 3. Continue the procedure with different numbers, alternating between adding-on one or two. Each time, start counting with the original number rather than with 1.

Variation: Have students predict how many will be left after one or two counters are taken away.

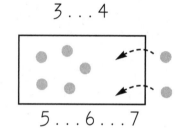

3 . . . 4

5 . . . 6 . . . 7

ACTIVITY 2 Counters in a Cup

Assemble a deck of playing cards that has face values of ace to 8 only. Student A draws a card from the deck and places it next to a cup. Then the student places in the cup a number of counters equal to the number on the drawn card. Record the number on a chart. Student B draws a card and places next to the cup a number of counters equal to the card number. Record this number on the chart. To find the total, begin counting with the total number of counters in the cup first, then continue counting those next to the cup. Record the total.

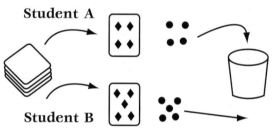

Student A

Student B

In Cup	Not in Cup	Total
4	5	9

ACTIVITY 3 Counter Trains

Provide students with 10 counters each. Have students build trains that are:

1 more than 5 ● ● ● ● ●   ●   3 more than 5 ● ● ● ● ●   ● ● ●

1 more than 6 ● ● ● ● ● ●   ●   2 more than 7 ● ● ● ● ● ● ●   ● ●

After each train is made, have students give the total.

Variation: Give students basic subtraction problems, such as: What number is 2 less than 7? Build trains to find the solutions.

Addition With Number Cards

These game-like activities offer you an engaging way to model for students how to use number cards for addition. The games also encourage students to practice on their own.

ACTIVITY 1   Two-Card Draw

Gather the whole class for a demonstration. Have a student select two number cards from a pile of cards with numbers 0–4. Display the cards for the class to see. Next, have the student draw simple illustrations of each number card on the chart. Have the student also fill in the total. After you have modeled the process several times with the class, have students complete the activity independently with their own set of cards, selecting two cards and completing a chart with a simple drawing and the total.

MATERIALS
2 sets of Student Response Cards (page 160)

Variation: Repeat as a classroom activity using cards 0–9.

Card 1	Card 2	Total
🐱 🐱	🐱 🐱 🐱 🐱	7

ACTIVITY 2   A Hill of Beans

Draw two cards. Have students say the sum. Depending on students' ability, use 0–5 cards or 0–9 cards.

MATERIALS
2 sets of bean cards (beans glued to 5-by 8-inch index cards as shown at left, or if beans are unavailable, drawings of beans)

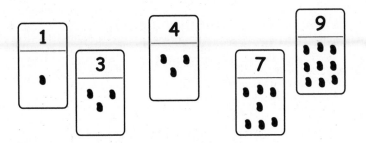

Variation 1: Use the cards to play a game. Three students are needed: a judge and two contestants. The judge presents two randomly selected cards. The contestant who responds most quickly with the sum scores a point.

Variation 2: As a whole-group activity, randomly select two cards and show the class. Students write an addition number sentence represented by the two cards.

Addition by Adding-on to 5 and 10

Students strengthen their addition skills by using 5 and 10 as an anchor in these activities. They represent the numbers they see on number cards with counters on a Ten-Frame chart to complete addition problems that have answers 5–10.

ACTIVITY 1 Adding-on to 5

Have one student draw a number card (0–9) from a bag and display it for all to see. Show students how to use counters on their Ten Frames to represent the number. Students may count to find the total.

Repeat this activity a few times. Then direct students to place five counters on the top row of their Ten Frames. Next, place number cards (0–5) in the bag. As a student draws a number card from the bag and displays it, the class adds that many counters to the five already on the Ten Frame. Ask students to "read" what's on their Ten Frame (for example, if they pull the 4 card, they may say "five plus four") and then figure out their total number of counters. Ask: *How did you get the total?* Encourage counting beginning with five.

MATERIALS
Copy of Ten Frame (page 155), bag, number cards 0–9, counters

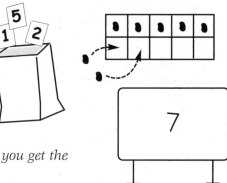

ACTIVITY 2 It's All About 10!

Directions: For each number 0–10 create a Ten Frame. Randomly display the frames and have students name the number that is represented by each one. Next, show a random mix of Ten Frames again, but have students name only the number of blank spaces they see. Then, randomly show Ten Frames a third time, and have students give the total for the counters and spaces (10). As a final step, show them the Ten Frames once again, and have students express the number of counters and spaces in the form of a number sentence. For example, they might say "six counters plus four blanks equals ten." Write the number sentences on the board—in this case, 6 + 4 = 10.

MATERIALS
Teacher-made Ten Frames (one for each number from 0–10 marked with dots or other objects)

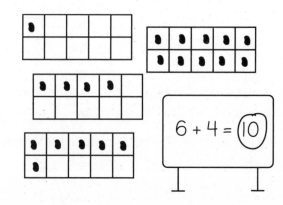

Complements of 10

The number 10 is a very useful number in math. Knowing the one-digit addends that add up to 10 is helpful for students as they improve at adding.

ACTIVITY   Adding Up to 10 With Counters and Charts

Put a number of Ten Frames facedown. Have students randomly select one and show the class. Ask students how many counters and blanks are shown. Write this information on the board in the form of a chart. Gradually, have students fill in the chart. See the sample below.

Counters	Blanks
2	8
4	6
5	5
3	7

MATERIALS

10 teacher-made Ten Frames that show a number of objects or counters (0–9), and board or chart paper. (Make copies of the Ten Frames reproducible on page 155, mark them with different numbers of objects, and mount the frames on colored construction paper or tagboard.)

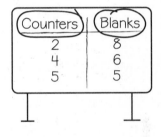

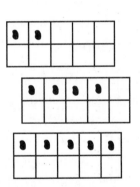

1. When you've finished the steps above, have students look at the chart as you ask questions about the pairs of numbers that make 10. Say: *If you have seven counters, how many spaces must you have to make ten?* Vary the question for five counters, three counters, nine counters, and so on.

2. Say: *Now let's see if you can figure out which pairs of numbers make ten without looking at the chart. When I say six, think of six counters. Then tell me the number of spaces that go with it to make ten.* Continue by varying the numbers you give them.

Variation: The above activity can be extended to do simple mental math. Select one of the teacher-made Ten Frames for all to see. Ask: *What number would we have if one more were added to the Ten Frame that you see?* When all the Ten Frames have been done, ask: *What number would we have if two more were added to the Ten Frame?* Continue with three more and so on.

Quick Counting to 5 and 10

Students use dice and coins to add-on to 5 and 10 quickly.

ACTIVITY 1   Rolling 5s

Students take turns rolling the two dice. The object is to
roll the highest total. Have students use tally marks to keep
score after each roll. One player passes the dice to the next.
The game is played until one player has a score of ten and wins.
Alternatively, you can stop the game
after 3 to 5 minutes. The winner
is the player with the highest score.

MATERIALS
Regular die, hand-adapted
die that has 5 on all six
sides (Use sticky circles
with five dots drawn on
them and place them on a
regular die.)

Score	
Lalit	Ray
⠇⠇⠇⠇⠇ ‖‖‖‖	⠇⠇⠇⠇⠇ ‖‖‖

ACTIVITY 2   Hidden Money

Have two students be contestants and one be a judge. Begin with a
nickel and four pennies. Each contestant lays out a nickel while
hiding in one hand the 4 pennies. When the judge says go, each
player takes out of hiding from 0–4 pennies and places them next
to their nickel. The opponent has to quickly add the value of the
coins. The first player to give the correct combined total of the money scores a point. The
judge decides who answered first and keeps score. The winner is the player who is the first
to score ten.

   Continue the game by introducing the dime. At this point, the players may take out of
hiding any amount of money that they wish for the other player to tally.

MATERIALS
A dime, a nickel, and 4
pennies for each player

Score	
Mira	Zona
⠇⠇⠇	⠇⠇⠇⠇

Name _____ Date _____

Story Problems You Can Solve

Directions: Here are some story problems. Use counters, the number line, or drawings to help you. Read carefully. After solving each, write your answer in the blank space.

1. Jeff is a dog lover. He has 4 dogs, and one of these dogs had 8 puppies. How many dogs does Jeff now have? _____ dogs

2. Jenny started a baseball card collection with 9 cards. She traded one of her valuable cards for 8 less valuable cards that had pictures of her favorite team. How many baseball cards does Jenny now have in her collection? (Remember, she had to trade in one of her cards.) _____ cards

3. Everett and Eddie shared a chocolate bar. Everett ate 4 pieces of the candy bar while Eddie finished it off by eating the remaining 6 pieces. How many pieces of chocolate were in the candy bar? _____ pieces

4. Kay and Kathy are playing a game. They roll a pair of dice to see who rolls the higher number and goes first. Kay rolls a 4 and a 5. Kathy rolls a 6 and a 2. Which player starts the game? _____

Directions: Read each problem below. Circle the correct answer.

5. Amos and Shirley decided to pool their money because they wanted to buy gum that cost 15 cents. Amos had 9 cents and Shirley had 7 cents. Did they have enough money together to buy the gum?   **Yes**   **No**

6. When Belinda went to her sister's volleyball game, the score was 6 for her sister's team, the Flyers, and 8 for the other team, the Jets. After watching 15 minutes more of the game, the Flyers scored 8 more points and the Jets scored 7 more points. Which team was ahead?   **Fliers**   **Jets**

Mastering Math Facts: Addition and Subtraction © 2009 Richard S. Piccirilli, Scholastic Teaching Resources

Name _____ Date _____

Writing Story Problems for Addition Facts

Directions: For each addition fact below, write a funny story problem. Be sure you have a question in your story.

············ **Example** ············

For 6 + 1 = 7, you could write: On Monday, Dan, the diamond cutter, cut 6 perfect diamonds for Cinderella. On Tuesday, Dan was so tired he could hardly work. He only cut 1 diamond for her. How many diamonds did Dan cut for Cinderella?

1. 5 + 2 = 7 _____
_____
_____

2. 6 + 8 = 14 _____
_____
_____

3. 9 + 7 = 16 _____
_____
_____

4. 8 + 0 = 8 _____
_____
_____

Directions: On the back of this sheet, draw a picture to show one of the story problems you wrote.

Mastering Math Facts: Addition and Subtraction © 2009 Richard S. Piccirilli, Scholastic Teaching Resources

Chapter 2

STRATEGIES

STEP 2   Teach Strategies to Make Addition Facts Easier

Strategies, which you might refer to as *tricks* or *shortcuts*, help students find patterns or special ways of attacking facts. Strategies are key to mastering the 100 addition and subtraction facts. After students use a strategy for a while, they know the number facts so naturally that they may not even remember when they didn't know the fact.

The strategies covered in this chapter include

- Zero the Hero (adding 0)

- Add 1 More (adding 1)

- Speedy 9s (adding 9)

- Doubles (adding a number to itself)

- Almost Doubles (using doubles to make almost-double facts easier)

- 10 Again (using 10 to make adding easier)

- Turnarounds (using the commutative property)

• What are the benefits of using strategies?

Using strategies employs thinking and reasoning. It makes number-fact learning easier and quicker while it contributes to long-term retention. At the same time, strategies help reduce mental fatigue and student workload. Fewer number facts need to be learned. Further, strategies help students create inventive ways to arrive at an answer when they don't immediately know an answer. Strategies take the boredom out of learning the 100 addition facts.

• How should strategies be taught?

You may have found that many of your students haven't mastered their facts and don't have any strategies to employ, even after they've completed textbook units. Why? Strategies need to become a real part of the learning process. Students need to see them, name them, talk about them, hear about them, appreciate their usefulness, and integrate them into their daily math vocabulary.

When it comes to teaching number facts, your focus should be on helping students

- Understand strategies and what they do

- Know the names for various strategies

- Use the strategy of their choice

- Internalize strategies

- Appreciate and value strategies

• Where do I begin?

You'll find it helpful to informally assess which facts students know and to look for their learning patterns, such as slowing down on addition facts with 0 or 9. Then teach the strategies that will support students, such as Zero the Hero (page 24) and the Speedy 9s strategy (page 26). After you've introduced a strategy, you can give students practice by having them complete a reproducible or work on facts independently, with a partner, or in a small group. You may also wish to start with strategy review pages, such as Detective Work: Match the Strategy (page 33). Depending on your students' needs, this page may serve as an informal assessment or as a review.

• What's in this chapter?

The chapter introduces a number of strategies to assist students in addition-fact mastery. Suggestions are given for applying each strategy, using concrete materials. Counters and ten frames are extremely useful as they present pictures that are worth a thousand words. You'll also find the opportunity to review the strategies with students and have them complete reproducibles to apply the different strategies—they will begin to see rewards as they work more efficiently.

The chapter ends with bulletin-board ideas to promote strategies. You may find it helpful to display a poster once you've introduced a strategy. Or, you may prefer to hang all the posters at once either at the beginning or end of your teaching of addition-fact strategies. Referring students to the posters regularly during your instruction can make the posters an important piece in addition-fact mastery. Simple names are offered for the various strategies. Of course, if you have a better name for a given strategy, use it with the class. Or, perhaps the class would like to invent their own names for the various strategies—a great way to encourage them to take further ownership of their learning.

Zero the Hero!

You make it s-0-0-0 easy!

When zero is added to a number, the answer is the same.

$8 + 0 =$

$+ 0$

10 AGAIN

Get to 10 again and again!

When sums are greater than 10, make a 10 out of one number, and add what's left to the 10.

$8 + 5 = 10 + 3 = 13$

$+ 10$

Zero the Hero: Teaching the Identity Property

Teaching the identity property for addition with "Zero the Hero" helps students see that adding zero makes things simple. Young children often think that adding zero to a number makes one more because they're adding something and thus supposed to get something larger. It may help students understand the ease of zero facts if you introduce other facts first so that they have a context for zero.

ACTIVITY Story Problems for the Identity Property

Start teaching zero number facts with story problems. Try both acting them out with students and having students use manipulatives to solve them. After you've modeled some story problems, ask children to make up their own story problems with zero.

Use the following problems as models. As you read each story problem, ask students to use counters to demonstrate the components. Practice until students don't require manipulatives to solve problems you give and problems they generate themselves.

1. Elmo had 2 cents in his pocket. His sister, Sally, had none. How many pennies did they have in all?

$$\left(1¢\right) + \left(1¢\right) + 0 = 2$$

2. In the first inning, our baseball team scored 4 runs. In the second inning, our team didn't score any runs. How many runs did our team score after 2 innings?

3. Vijay's cat, caught 3 mice the first week. The next week, she caught 1. The week after that, she didn't catch any. How many mice did the cat catch in all?

4. On Monday, it rained. On Tuesday, it was sunny. On Wednesday, it rained again. On how many days did it rain?

5. At the zoo, Ali saw that there were no monkeys in the yellow cage, but there were 5 monkeys in the orange cage. How many monkeys did Ali see?

6. Dad didn't catch any fish on a recent camping trip. Mom caught 6 on the trip and Nan caught 7. How many fish were caught together?

Name _____ Date _____

Zero the Hero

Directions: Zip through these addition facts by finding the correct sum.
Remember what it means when we add our hero, zero.

0 + 2	7 + 0	0 + 6	0 + 3	5 + 0	0 + 7
9 + 0	4 + 0	0 + 1	0 + 8	2 + 0	0 + 5
0 + 4	6 + 0	0 + 9	1 + 0	8 + 0	0 + 0

Explain why zero is a hero.

_____

_____

Mastering Math Facts: Addition and Subtraction © 2009 Richard S. Piccirilli, Scholastic Teaching Resources

Add 1 More: An Adding-on Strategy

These activities help students internalize the strategy of adding-on one more.

ACTIVITY 1   Adding 1 With Number Cards

Randomly display a number card, and have students tell the number that is one more than the number on the card. Be sure to have students summarize the strategy: *When you add one to a number, the answer is the next number!*

MATERIALS
Ten index cards, numbered 0–9, or use Student Response Cards (page 160)

Variation 1: Instead of using cards, use your fingers as the base number to which you want students to add one. For example: Show three fingers. Ask what one more would be. Students respond.

Variation 2: Give a number orally and ask the student or class to add-on to that number.

Variation 3: Present a number card at random while students respond with one more using either a 3 x 5 card like the teacher's or a set of Student Response Cards.

ACTIVITY 2   Adding 1 With Flash Cards

For this activity, have students work alone or with a partner. Have the student(s) pull out all the flash cards that follow the Add-on One More strategy, such as 0 + 1, 1 + 1, 2 + 1, and then practice the facts.

MATERIALS
Flash cards containing all 100 addition facts

| 0
+ 1 | 1
+ 0 | 1
+ 1 | 1
+ 2 | 2
+ 1 | 3
+ 1 | 1
+ 3 | 1
+ 4 | 4
+ 1 |

Speedy 9s: The Strategy to Add a 9

These activities show students how to employ the Speedy 9s strategy using manipulatives.

ACTIVITY 1   Speedy 9s With Ten Frames

Using Ten-Frames and counters, have students model $9 + 5$, $8 + 9$, and $9 + 6$ one at a time.

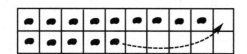

MATERIALS
10 copies of Ten-Ten Frames (page 155), counters.

After examining each set of Ten Frames, ask: *How can you quickly tell what the sum is for each? Explain.* Have students explain why one counter was moved to make a ten. Guide students to see that when a number is added to 9, the digit in ones place of the answer is one less than the number being added to 9. Ask: *Can anyone predict the ones-place digit in nine plus four?*

ACTIVITY 2   Speedy 9s in Action

Write the examples below on the board.

$$\begin{array}{r} 9 \\ + ⑶ \\ \hline 1② \end{array} \qquad \begin{array}{r} 9 \\ + ⑸ \\ \hline 1④ \end{array} \qquad \begin{array}{r} ⑧ \\ + 9 \\ \hline 1⑦ \end{array} \qquad \begin{array}{r} ④ \\ + 9 \\ \hline 1③ \end{array}$$

MATERIALS
Chalkboard or whiteboard

Ask: *How does the digit in the ones place of the answer relate to the number added to 9?* (It's one less.) Next, have students solve the first five problems below, and write the answers on the board. Then have volunteers quickly answer the remaining five problems.

1. $\begin{array}{r} 9 \\ + 6 \\ \hline 1\bigcirc \end{array}$	2. $\begin{array}{r} 2 \\ + 9 \\ \hline 1\bigcirc \end{array}$	3. $\begin{array}{r} 9 \\ + 4 \\ \hline 1\bigcirc \end{array}$	4. $\begin{array}{r} 7 \\ + 9 \\ \hline 1\bigcirc \end{array}$	5. $\begin{array}{r} 9 \\ + 9 \\ \hline 1\bigcirc \end{array}$
6. $\begin{array}{r} 9 \\ + 5 \\ \hline 1\bigcirc \end{array}$	7. $\begin{array}{r} 9 \\ + 3 \\ \hline 1\bigcirc \end{array}$	8. $\begin{array}{r} 9 \\ + 8 \\ \hline 1\bigcirc \end{array}$	9. $\begin{array}{r} 1 \\ + 9 \\ \hline 1\bigcirc \end{array}$	10. $\begin{array}{r} 9 \\ + 2 \\ \hline 1\bigcirc \end{array}$

Variation: Present the 9 combinations orally to see how quickly students can respond.

10 Again: The Value of Making Tens

Everyone loves the number 10 because working with it is easy. Teach students that when they add basic facts, they should look for ways to get to 10 again and again to speed up work. This activity helps students identify and use the 10 Again strategy.

ACTIVITY 10 Again With Frames and Counters

Have students show addition facts by moving counters to make tens. Begin by modeling with counters on the Ten-Ten Frame: 8 + 5 = ? Ask: *What's a quick way of finding out how many objects we have on our frame?*

MATERIALS
Ten-Ten Frames (page 155) and counters

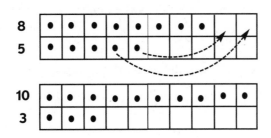

Show students how to move two counters up to make a ten. Ask: *What's left?* Point out that once we have 10, three are left. So, add 10 and three to get 13. Ask: *Why do you think it's helpful to get to ten over and over again?* Guide students to see that making a 10 and adding-on what's left is easier to figure out than the original combination.

Choose some examples below to give students practice in the 10 Again strategy, using counters and a Ten-Ten Frame. Let them work on page 28 independently.

* 6 + 5	7 + 4	8 + 3
* 6 + 6	7 + 5	8 + 4
* 6 + 7	* 6 + 7	8 + 5
6 + 8	* 7 + 7	8 + 6
* 6 + 9	* 7 + 8	* 8 + 7
	* 7 + 9	* 8 + 8
		* 8 + 9

* Let students know that for these combinations, there may be other strategies that are simpler to use than 10 Again. It is important for students to see that for some addition facts, they may choose the quickest among multiple strategies.

Name _____ Date _____

10 Is a Friend: Using 10 Again

Directions: Look at the example with number combinations that make 10 easily. Then answer the problems using 10 Again.

Example

$$8 \ (+ 2) = \quad 10$$

$$\underline{+ \ 5 \ (- 2)} = \quad \underline{+ \ 3}$$

$$ \quad 13$$

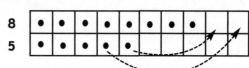

Directions: Some of the facts below are easy to solve with the 10-Again strategy. Circle them and answer them.

1.

$$\begin{array}{r} 4 \\ + \ 5 \\ \hline \end{array} \qquad \begin{array}{r} 8 \\ + \ 3 \\ \hline \end{array} \qquad \begin{array}{r} 3 \\ + \ 4 \\ \hline \end{array} \qquad \begin{array}{r} 4 \\ + \ 7 \\ \hline \end{array}$$

2.

$$\begin{array}{r} 7 \\ + \ 5 \\ \hline \end{array} \qquad \begin{array}{r} 2 \\ + \ 6 \\ \hline \end{array} \qquad \begin{array}{r} 5 \\ + \ 8 \\ \hline \end{array} \qquad \begin{array}{r} 3 \\ + \ 8 \\ \hline \end{array}$$

3.

$$\begin{array}{r} 8 \\ + \ 5 \\ \hline \end{array} \qquad \begin{array}{r} 5 \\ + \ 3 \\ \hline \end{array} \qquad \begin{array}{r} 8 \\ + \ 4 \\ \hline \end{array} \qquad \begin{array}{r} 7 \\ + \ 5 \\ \hline \end{array}$$

4.

$$\begin{array}{r} 6 \\ + \ 3 \\ \hline \end{array} \qquad \begin{array}{r} 6 \\ + \ 8 \\ \hline \end{array} \qquad \begin{array}{r} 2 \\ + \ 7 \\ \hline \end{array} \qquad \begin{array}{r} 4 \\ + \ 8 \\ \hline \end{array}$$

Mastering Math Facts: Addition and Subtraction © 2009 Richard S. Piccirilli, Scholastic Teaching Resources

Neighbors Helping Neighbors: Discovering Almost-Doubles

Once students know their doubles facts, using almost-doubles is a useful strategy. To help students remember the strategy, we show how almost-doubles facts are like neighbors.

ACTIVITY   The Almost-Doubles Strategy

Review doubles facts, such as 0 + 0, 1 + 1, 2 + 2, and so on. Then tell students that they will look at some "neighbors" of doubles to use with counters.

MATERIALS
Counters

Invite students to share what they know about neighbors. Remind them that because neighbors live close to each other, they help each other. Neighbor numbers are 0 and 1, 1 and 2, 2 and 3, 3 and 4, and so forth. Neighbor numbers make almost-double combinations: 0 + 1 (not 0 + 0 or 1 + 1), 1 + 2 (not 1 + 1 or 2 + 2), and so forth.

Model solving a problem using the almost-double strategy: In the equation 6 + 7 = ?, 7 is a neighbor number of 6. So we think, 6 + 6 plus 1 more makes a total of 13. Ask: *Can you think of the doubles fact for 6's neighbor, 7?* (7 + 7 is 14) *Then take one away, and what's left?* (13) In the case of 6 + 7, you can use the strategy two ways: You can think of 6 as an almost-double of 7, to which you add one. Or, you can think of 7 as an almost-double of 6, from which you subtract one.

Example

Lay out three counters. Put four counters below the three counters.

3 ● ● ●   3 ● ● ●

=   + ●   or 6 + 1 = 7

4 ● ● ● ●   3 ● ● ●

Ask: *How can you use the two sets of counters to find the sum of 3 + 4?* (You can quickly see two rows of 3, which you know is 6. Then you add one more to get 7).

Explain how you can check that your answer is right. Point out that students know the double fact, 3 + 3. Since 4 is a neighbor of 3, you add one more. You can also choose the higher double fact, 4 + 4. You know the sum is 8 and then you take one away. In this case, you're looking at 3 as a neighbor 4.

Practice • With students, model how to use counters and the Almost-Doubles strategy to figure out the following equations:

5 + 4   6 + 5   8 + 7   9 + 8   7 + 6

Turnarounds: Teaching the Commutative Property

You can easily model the commutative property with role-playing and manipulatives. This will help students internalize the fact that changing the order of the addends doesn't change the answer. Turnarounds can be a time-saver on students' journey toward number-fact mastery.

ACTIVITY   Turnaround Strategy Role Play

Have students role-play the following story problem:

> Mr. Quigley asked three helpers to carry books to Ms. Locke's class. Mr. Quigley realized that the books were heavy, so he chose four more helpers to carry the books. How many helpers did Mr. Quigley need?

As you read the story problem, have three students stand in front. As more helpers are described, have four more students come up. Ask each group to line up separately. You can represent the students' model pictorially by making stick figures on the board or on screen, like so:

$$3 \quad + \quad 4 \quad = 7$$

Ask: *How many students did we call up first? (3) How many students did we call up next? (4) What's the total number of students needed to help? (7)*

Say: *Suppose I called up the four helpers first and I called up the three helpers next.* (Role-play this.) What's the total number of helpers now? (It's still 7.) Tell students that addition facts can "turn around" and have the same answer; it doesn't matter which number comes first. Show this drawing below the first drawing to reinforce the concept of turnarounds.

$$4 \quad + \quad 3 \quad = 7$$

Variation: Ask students to use counters to model the turnarounds in the story. Find more ideas for modeling turnarounds on page 31 and activities for practicing with the strategy on page 32.

Using Turnarounds:
Other Ideas to Teach the Commutative Property

These demonstrations give students experience using different materials to represent the commutative property of addition—the turnaround strategy. Try the role-play activity on the previous page first.

ACTIVITY   Turnaround Demonstrations

Discuss how the turnaround, reversing the order of the numbers, does not change the answer in addition facts.

MATERIALS

Ten Frames (page 155), dominoes, graph paper, colored pencils, beads on a wire, picture cards of dominoes.

1. Draw: Have students draw a picture for 6 + 3 and 3 + 6, such as:

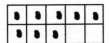 6 + 3 = 9

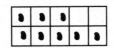 3 + 6 = 9

2. Use Ten Frames: Have students use counters on Ten Frames to show 5 + 3 and 3 + 5.

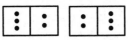

3. Demonstrate with Dominoes: Have students find matching dominoes to show 3 + 2 and 2 + 3.

4. Use Squared Paper: With colored pencils on graph paper, ask students to show 4 + 5 and 5 + 4.

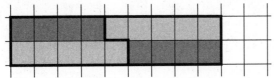

5. Show Beads on a Wire: Have students move beads to show 4 + 3 and 3 + 4.

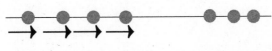

Playing Around With Turnarounds

By using the commutative property, the workload of learning the 100 addition facts is reduced by 50 percent. A bonus in having students interact with turnaround number facts is that they are being exposed to number facts in thoughtful ways that encourage practice and ease memorization at a later date.

ACTIVITY 1   Pairing-Up Turnarounds

On the board, write 10 matching fact pairs (such as 5 + 7 = 12, 7 + 5 = 12, 6 + 0 = 6, 0 + 6 = 6, and so on). You should have a total of 20 equations in random order for all students to see. Ask students to study the equations to find the matching pairs. Call students up to highlight the matches by framing each pair in a different color and shape (such as circling, boxing, or putting triangles around the two equations that match).

$$\begin{array}{cc} 4 \\ + 2 \end{array} \quad \begin{array}{cc} 3 \\ + 5 \end{array} \quad \begin{array}{cc} 0 \\ + 8 \end{array} \quad \begin{array}{cc} 7 \\ + 3 \end{array} \quad \begin{array}{cc} 5 \\ + 6 \end{array} \quad \begin{array}{cc} 2 \\ + 4 \end{array} \quad \begin{array}{cc} 6 \\ + 3 \end{array} \quad \begin{array}{cc} 7 \\ + 2 \end{array} \quad \begin{array}{cc} 5 \\ + 3 \end{array} \quad \begin{array}{cc} 3 \\ + 7 \end{array}$$

ACTIVITY 2   Turnaround Concentration

Play a game like Concentration, in which each player has to match the turnaround pairs. Use 10 matching pairs of flash cards. In rows, put the twenty cards facedown. Have students take turns flipping over cards. If the player finds a match, he or she keeps the pair and tries again. Students alternate until all the cards are turned over. The winner is the player with the most matches.

MATERIALS
10 pairs of addition facts flash cards

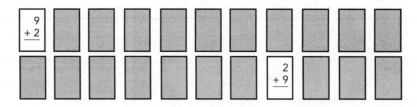

ACTIVITY 3   Name That Fact

Give students oral practice with turnarounds. First, say an addition fact, and have students write the turnaround fact. Then reverse roles. You'll write an addition fact on the board, and then call on a volunteer to say the turnaround fact out loud. You may also ask students to say the turnaround fact chorally as you finish writing each example.

For example, call out the fact 3 + 6 = 9 (Students write *6 + 3 = 9*).
Write: *7 + 4 = 11* (Students call out the fact 4 + 7 = 11)

Name _____ Date _____

Detective Work: Match the Strategy

Directions: Choose an addition combination from the box below. Which strategy is best for solving the problem? Write the addition fact in one column. Continue until you have used all the addition facts. Remember, some number facts match with more than one strategy. Just choose one. The first three are done for you.

Zero the Hero	Add 1 More	Almost-Doubles	Speedy 9s	10 Again
0 + 5	5 + 1			8 + 5

Addition Combinations

8 + 5	0 + 5	5 + 1	7 + 8	6 + 7	4 + 9
1 + 6	7 + 6	0 + 3	0 + 4	9 + 5	2 + 1
0 + 0	8 + 1	5 + 7	9 + 7	2 + 0	0 + 8
7 + 9	8 + 3	4 + 8	3 + 9	8 + 7	8 + 6
6 + 8	1 + 4	9 + 6	3 + 4	6 + 1	5 + 6

Mastering Math Facts: Addition and Subtraction © 2009 Richard S. Piccirilli, Scholastic Teaching Resources

More Detective Work: Addition Strategy Practice

These review activities give students practice in deciding which strategy to use for addition facts

MATERIALS
Addition facts flash cards, index cards

ACTIVITY 1 Flash Card Strategy Review 1

Rather than use a reproducible as review, try a whole-group activity in which you show the class a flash card and ask students to identify the most appropriate strategy. You may want to have the strategy names and tips posted as a reminder (see pages 37–38, Advertise Your Strategies). As it comes up, discuss the fact that more than one strategy may fit some addition facts.

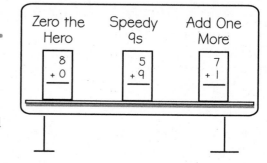

ACTIVITY 2 Flash Card Strategy Review 2

Write the names of five strategies on the board. Show students flash cards of addition facts. As a card is shown, call on a volunteer to place the flash card under the appropriate strategy. Then survey the class to ask how many would use that strategy to figure out the answer or which strategy could be used instead. Also assess how many students know the answer without employing any strategy.

ACTIVITY 3 Flash Card Strategy Review 3

Do strategy review in a small group or with individual students. In this case, write a strategy heading on each of five 3- by 5-inch index cards. Display the cards in a row on the table. Take a stack of addition flash cards and place it face down. Have a student turn over the first flash card from the stack and decide where it belongs, based on which strategy is best suited for solving the problem.

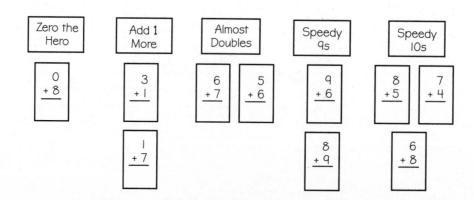

Appreciating Number-Fact Strategies

This demonstration helps emphasize to students that knowing number-fact strategies helps them quickly recall at least 50, if not more, number facts without hard work.

ACTIVITY 100 Facts—Strategy Overview

Give one direction at a time. If you have students work independently, direct them to complete one direction before going on to the next. For each strategy, ask students to circle and write answers to all of the addition combinations they can solve with:

1. Zero the Hero
2. Add 1 More
3. Speedy 9s
4. 10 Again
5. Almost Doubles
6. Doubles

When the assignment is complete, ask students to raise their hands to show how many facts they circled. Ask: *40 or more facts? 50 or more? More than 60?*

MATERIALS

100-problem addition fact test (any practice test, pages 87 to 91); individual copies and transparency/digital copy to use on screen

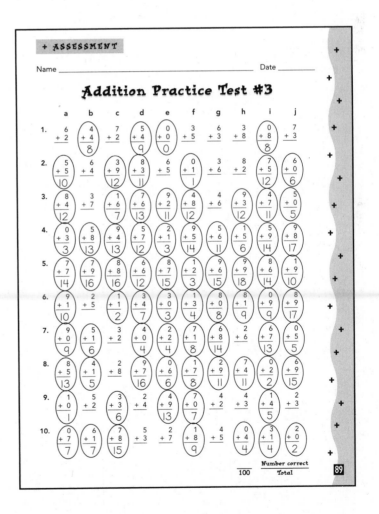

Visualizing the Addition Strategies

When students shade in the Addition-Subtraction Tables, they create visual patterns that reinforce the six key strategies they've studied: Addition with 0, 1, 9, and 10, doubling, and almost-doubling.

ACTIVITY 1 Picturing the Strategy • Demonstration

On screen, display the Addition-Subtraction Table. For each addition strategy you teach, shade in the sums on one of the charts. Using page 158, you can show and compare six strategies at once.

MATERIALS
Copy of pages 61 (single large chart) and 158 (six small charts) for each student

ACTIVITY 2 Picturing the Strategy • Practice

Make copies of the Addition-Subtraction Table (page 61). Have students shade in the chart as they study each strategy. Using a different color for each set of facts will support memorization.

ACTIVITY 3 Making an All-in-One Chart

Have students combine all of their strategies onto one large chart (colored pencils will help them distinguish the different sets of facts and see where the facts overlap). They will be amazed at how many of the 100 addition facts are covered by strategies!

+	0	1	2	3	4	5	6	7	8	9
0	0	1	2	3	4	5	6	7	8	9
1	1	2	3	4	5	6	7	8	9	10
2	2	3	4	5	6	7	8	9	10	11
3	3	4	5	6	7	8	9	10	11	12
4	4	5	6	7	8	9	10	11	12	13
5	5	6	7	8	9	10	11	12	13	14
6	6	7	8	9	10	11	12	13	14	15
7	7	8	9	10	11	12	13	14	15	16
8	8	9	10	11	12	13	14	15	16	17
9	9	10	11	12	13	14	15	16	17	18

Zero the Hero

+	0	1	2	3	4	5	6	7	8	9
0	0	1	2	3	4	5	6	7	8	9
1	1	2	3	4	5	6	7	8	9	10
2	2	3	4	5	6	7	8	9	10	11
3	3	4	5	6	7	8	9	10	11	12
4	4	5	6	7	8	9	10	11	12	13
5	5	6	7	8	9	10	11	12	13	14
6	6	7	8	9	10	11	12	13	14	15
7	7	8	9	10	11	12	13	14	15	16
8	8	9	10	11	12	13	14	15	16	17
9	9	10	11	12	13	14	15	16	17	18

Add 1 More

+	0	1	2	3	4	5	6	7	8	9
0	0	1	2	3	4	5	6	7	8	9
1	1	2	3	4	5	6	7	8	9	10
2	2	3	4	5	6	7	8	9	10	11
3	3	4	5	6	7	8	9	10	11	12
4	4	5	6	7	8	9	10	11	12	13
5	5	6	7	8	9	10	11	12	13	14
6	6	7	8	9	10	11	12	13	14	15
7	7	8	9	10	11	12	13	14	15	16
8	8	9	10	11	12	13	14	15	16	17
9	9	10	11	12	13	14	15	16	17	18

Speedy 9s

+	0	1	2	3	4	5	6	7	8	9
0	0	1	2	3	4	5	6	7	8	9
1	1	2	3	4	5	6	7	8	9	10
2	2	3	4	5	6	7	8	9	10	11
3	3	4	5	6	7	8	9	10	11	12
4	4	5	6	7	8	9	10	11	12	13
5	5	6	7	8	9	10	11	12	13	14
6	6	7	8	9	10	11	12	13	14	15
7	7	8	9	10	11	12	13	14	15	16
8	8	9	10	11	12	13	14	15	16	17
9	9	10	11	12	13	14	15	16	17	18

10 Again

+	0	1	2	3	4	5	6	7	8	9
0	0	1	2	3	4	5	6	7	8	9
1	1	2	3	4	5	6	7	8	9	10
2	2	3	4	5	6	7	8	9	10	11
3	3	4	5	6	7	8	9	10	11	12
4	4	5	6	7	8	9	10	11	12	13
5	5	6	7	8	9	10	11	12	13	14
6	6	7	8	9	10	11	12	13	14	15
7	7	8	9	10	11	12	13	14	15	16
8	8	9	10	11	12	13	14	15	16	17
9	9	10	11	12	13	14	15	16	17	18

Doubles

+	0	1	2	3	4	5	6	7	8	9
0	0	1	2	3	4	5	6	7	8	9
1	1	2	3	4	5	6	7	8	9	10
2	2	3	4	5	6	7	8	9	10	11
3	3	4	5	6	7	8	9	10	11	12
4	4	5	6	7	8	9	10	11	12	13
5	5	6	7	8	9	10	11	12	13	14
6	6	7	8	9	10	11	12	13	14	15
7	7	8	9	10	11	12	13	14	15	16
8	8	9	10	11	12	13	14	15	16	17
9	9	10	11	12	13	14	15	16	17	18

Almost Doubles

Mastering Math Facts: Addition and Subtraction © 2009 Richard S. Piccirilli, Scholastic Teaching Resources

Advertise the Strategies

Underscore the importance and value of addition-fact strategies by designing an attractive bulletin board with posters that promote number-fact learning. Use the strategies as named in this book or, alternatively, invite your class to make up their own names for the strategies. What's important is that each strategy has a name, and students know the strategies for their addition facts.

ACTIVITY Strategy Posters

Use the following as models for posters to display in your classroom.

MATERIALS
Chart paper or posterboard, markers

Zero the Hero!

You make it s·0·0·0 easy!

When zero is added to a number, the answer is the same number.

$8 + 0 = 8$

+ 0

Add 1 More

You get the next number!

When one is added to another number, the answer is one more than the number.

$6 + 1 = 7$

+ 1

Speedy 9s

Save time with 9!

When nine is added to a number, the number in ones place is one less than the number being added to the nine.

$9 + 6 = 15$
$8 + 9 = 17$

+ 9

10 AGAIN

Get to 10 again and again!

When sums are greater than 10, make a 10 out of one number, and add what's left to the 10.

$$8 + 5 = 10 + 3 = 13$$

+ 10

Almost-Doubles

are numbers that get help from neighbor numbers

When adding two numbers that are neighbors, remember your doubles fact and add or subtract 1.

$$7 + 8 = 7 + 7 + 1 = 15 \text{ or}$$
$$7 + 8 = 8 + 8 - 1 = 15$$

−1 or +1

Turnarounds

Turn them around and the sum is the same!

When adding two numbers, turn them around to learn another number fact.

$$3 + 4 = 7$$
$$4 + 3 = 7$$

Chapter 3

PRACTICE

Practice Addition Facts to Think Strategically

Practice gives students opportunities to reason, understand, and use strategies with number-fact learning. Practice should not be confused with drill—the fourth and next step in this approach. Practice employs thinking, while drills focus on making facts automatic.

As students use number facts in routine and nonroutine problem situations, they develop a relationship with number pairs and gain a sense of about how much the answer should be. With practice, students gradually acquire precision in their answers, which moves them along the path to mastery.

- What are the benefits of practice?

Practice provides many experiences with numbers that help students develop intuition about how numbers behave. It builds number sense and helps students see how useful number facts can be in solving problems.

Practice helps students:

1. Develop a relationship with number pairs and their corresponding sum. For example, as one addend gets larger and the other gets smaller by the same amount, the answers are the same.

2. Compare number facts. For example, 5 + 2 has a larger answer sum than 5 + 1. Students should know that the answer will be greater than 5 but less than 10.

3. Create opportunities for flexible thinking. Students build relationships among the facts. For example, since 7 + 5 makes 12, then 5 + 7 makes 12. In another example, if you take 1 from the 7 and give it to the 5, you have 6 + 6. The combination 7 + 5 can also be broken down as (5 + 2) + 5 and rebuilt as (5 + 5) + 2. In this case, students learn to see a number as the sum of its parts.

4. Estimate the range in which the answer falls by determining whether the sum is less than or more than 10.

5. Relate addition to subtraction. Students see this, for example, when they find the missing addend.

6. Learn when, how, and why it is best to use number facts.

7. Realize that knowing their basic number facts enables them to answer more easily and quickly than they would by counting.

- What are the guidelines for giving students practice?

Students should have the necessary prerequisites before they begin practice. You should ensure that students have a strong understanding of the meaning of number facts and the strategies to unlock their solutions. Schedule practice for short but frequent sessions. You'll find it best to distribute practice over a period of time and to include activities that are interesting and engaging to the children in your class.

• What's in this chapter?

This chapter begins with problem solving, which serves as a context for developing number-fact learning. Students solve and then write story problems. Students also solve problems by manipulating numbers and searching for numbers to answer questions. These activities teach students uses for addition facts.

The next set of activities focuses on missing numbers that emphasize patterns and give students practice with the commutative property. Again, students interact with combinations and answers while strengthening the number relationship that creates an addition fact.

There are also three practice pages in this chapter (pages 47–49) that ask students to compare addition facts. In the process, students continue to see the relationship between the numbers that form facts. Students will also call on strategies to make quick judgments as they compare combinations.

The next four pages of the chapter encourage flexible and critical thinking with exercises that help students decompose and recompose numbers. Students learn how to construct an answer to a number fact they may have forgotten. Following are review activities that emphasize strategic thinking for faster recall.

The chapter finishes with suggestions you can use for teaching with triangular flash cards and with using the chart of 100 facts. Flash-card activities help students reinforce concepts related to patterns, odd and even answers, number families, and strategies. The chart with 100 addition/subtraction facts helps students find patterns and think resourcefully about number facts.

The chapter provides a good deal of practice. With these many different kinds of number-adding experiences, you should see students begin to memorize their addition facts.

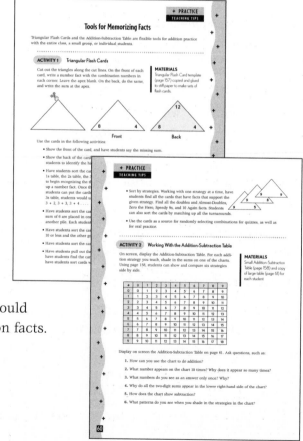

Name _____ Date _____

Number, Please

Directions: Read each story problem and answer it with a number. Show the addition fact you used.

········ **Example** ········

1. How old is my sister? I am 8 years old. My sister is 6 years older than me.
   __14__ years old

$$
\begin{array}{r}
8 \\
+ 6 \\
\hline
14
\end{array}
$$

2. On the school playground, Roberto jumped rope 7 times in a row. Juan jumped 9 times in a row. How many times did both boys jump in a row?

   _____ times

3. Jason and Al are brothers. Jason worked 8 hours cutting grass. Al worked 3 hours cutting grass. How many hours did they work all together?

   _____ hours

4. When I was 3 feet tall, my brother was 2 feet taller than me. How tall was my brother?

   _____ feet tall

5. On the first day, Angela read 9 pages of her new book. By the second day she was on page 14. How many pages did she read on the second day?

   _____ pages

6. Jenny's pet gerbil, Rusty, runs in his wheel every day. One day, he ran for 5 minutes, stopped for a drink of water, and then ran again for 8 minutes. How much time did Rusty run on his wheel that day?

   _____ minutes

7. On the first day of basketball practice, Emelio made 9 baskets in a row. The next day Emelio made another 9 in a row. How many baskets did he make in two days?

   _____ baskets

8. Tia frosted 8 chocolate cupcakes and 9 vanilla cupcakes. How many cupcakes did Tia frost?

   _____ cupcakes

Name _____ Date _____

Writing Story Problems

Directions: For each number combination below, write a funny story problem. Make sure that you have a question in your story. Draw a picture to help you.

········· **Example** ·········

3 + 2 Fido, the talking dog, told his friend that he ate 3 doggie treats yesterday and 2 doggie treats this morning. How many doggie treats did Fido eat?

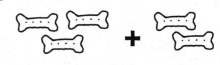

1. 4 + 5 _____

_____

_____

2. 7 + 0 _____

_____

_____

3. 6 + 5 _____

_____

_____

4. 8 + 9 _____

_____

_____

Mastering Math Facts: Addition and Subtraction © 2009 Richard S. Piccirilli, Scholastic Teaching Resources

Name _____ Date _____

Sum Circle Puzzle

Directions: Cut out the circles at the bottom of the page. Arrange them in the open circles of the puzzle so that the sum is 8 when you add the three numbers across and also 8 when you add the three numbers down. When you finish, write your solution in A.

Now arrange the number circles so that the sum is 9 each way. Write your answer in B. Next, try making the sum 10 each way and write your answer in C.

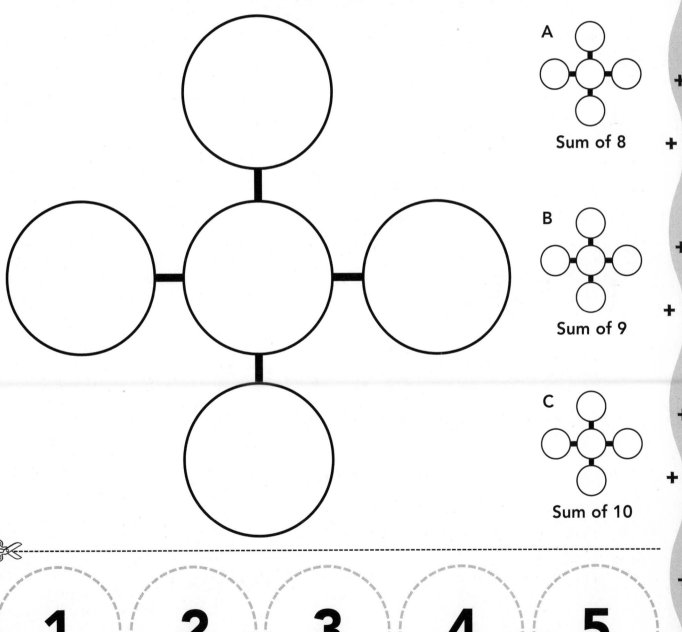

A

Sum of 8

B

Sum of 9

C

Sum of 10

1   2   3   4   5

Name _____ Date _____

Number Search

Directions: Look in the box for the numbers that answer the question.

1	7	5	6	4	9	0

······· **Example** ·······

1. What two numbers have a sum of 10?   __1__ , __9__ **and** __6__ , __4__
   (Find two sets.)

2. What two numbers have a sum of 13?   ___ , ___ **and** ___ , ___
   (Find two sets.)

3. What two numbers have a sum of 1?   ___ , ___

4. What two numbers have a sum of 9?   ___ , ___ **and** ___ , ___
   (Find two sets.)

5. What two numbers have a sum of 14?   ___ , ___

6. What two numbers have a sum of 15?   ___ , ___

7. What two numbers have a sum of 16?   ___ , ___

8. What three numbers have a sum of 15?   ___ , ___ , ___
   (Find 3 sets.)

and ___ , ___ , ___

and ___ , ___ , ___

Mastering Math Facts: Addition and Subtraction © 2009 Richard S. Piccirilli, Scholastic Teaching Resources

Name _____ Date _____

What's Missing? Part 1

Directions: Look at the charts below. The top of each column shows a sum.
Below are combinations of numbers that add up to that sum. Some numbers are
missing! Write the missing addend to complete each combination.

Sum: 1	Sum: 2	Sum: 3	Sum: 4	Sum: 5
1 + _____	2 + _____	_____ + 0	4 + _____	5 + _____
	1 + _____	_____ + 1	3 + _____	_____ + 1
	0 + _____	1 + _____	2 + _____	3 + _____
		0 + _____	_____ + 3	2 + _____
			_____ + 4	4 + _____
				0 + _____

Sum: 6	Sum: 7	Sum: 8	Sum: 9	Sum: 10
6 + _____	_____ + 0	_____ + 0	9 + _____	9 + _____
5 + _____	_____ + 1	7 + _____	_____ + 1	_____ + 2
_____ + 2	_____ + 2	_____ + 2	7 + _____	7 + _____
_____ + 3	4 + _____	5 + _____	_____ + 4	6 + _____
_____ + 4	3 + _____	_____ + 4	5 + _____	5 + _____
1 + _____	_____ + 5	3 + _____	_____ + 5	_____ + 6
_____ + 6	_____ + 6	_____ + 6	3 + _____	_____ + 7
	_____ + 7	1 + _____	2 + _____	2 + _____
		0 + _____	_____ + 8	1 + _____

What helped you to fill in some of your answers? (Write your answer on the back of
this page.)

Name _____ Date _____

What's Missing? Part 2

Directions: Look at the charts below. The top of each column shows a sum. Below are combinations of numbers that add up to that sum. Some numbers are missing! Write the missing addend to complete each combination.

Sum: 11	Sum: 12	Sum: 13	Sum: 14
9 + _____	_____ + 3	9 + _____	_____ + 5
_____ + 3	_____ + 4	8 + _____	_____ + 6
7 + _____	7 + _____	_____ + 6	_____ + 7
6 + _____	6 + _____	_____ + 7	6 + _____
_____ + 6	5 + _____	_____ + 8	5 + _____
_____ + 7	8 + _____	4 + _____	
3 + _____	9 + _____		
2 + _____			

Sum: 15	Sum: 16	Sum: 17	Sum: 18
9 + _____	7 + _____	9 + _____	_____ + 9
_____ + 7	8 + _____	_____ + 8	
_____ + 8	_____ + 7		
_____ + 6			

What patterns did you notice that helped you fill in the blanks?

_____

_____

Name _____ Date _____

Point It Out!

Directions: Point out the combination that has the larger sum by filling in the circle with an arrow (→) that points to the larger sum. If the sum of each combination is the same, fill in the circle with an equal sign (=).

Examples

3 + 1 ← 1 + 2

6 + 2 → 2 + 7

4 + 1 = 5 + 0

1. 7 + 6 ◯ 5 + 7

2. 4 + 3 ◯ 4 + 4

3. 9 + 1 ◯ 6 + 3

4. 8 + 5 ◯ 6 + 8

5. 8 + 8 ◯ 9 + 6

6. 0 + 7 ◯ 6 + 1

7. 4 + 7 ◯ 7 + 4

8. 3 + 8 ◯ 7 + 5

9. 8 + 0 ◯ 0 + 8

10. 6 + 6 ◯ 7 + 6

11. 0 + 0 ◯ 1 + 1

12. 7 + 6 ◯ 8 + 5

Name _____ Date _____

A, B, C:
Which Is the Largest of the Three?

Directions: In each item, put a check mark ✓ after the A, B or C to show which addition combination has the largest sum.

1. A _____ 6 + 8

    B _____ 7 + 9

    C _____ 8 + 9

5. A _____ 6 + 1

    B _____ 8 + 0

    C _____ 5 + 2

9. A _____ 9 + 7

    B _____ 7 + 8

    C _____ 9 + 8

2. A _____ 2 + 3

    B _____ 6 + 1

    C _____ 4 + 2

6. A _____ 6 + 5

    B _____ 6 + 4

    C _____ 3 + 7

10. A _____ 2 + 2

    B _____ 3 + 3

    C _____ 3 + 7

3. A _____ 7 + 8

    B _____ 6 + 9

    C _____ 8 + 8

7. A _____ 4 + 3

    B _____ 7 + 2

    C _____ 2 + 8

11. A _____ 4 + 8

    B _____ 7 + 4

    C _____ 5 + 6

4. A _____ 7 + 3

    B _____ 6 + 2

    C _____ 4 + 5

8. A _____ 9 + 1

    B _____ 3 + 8

    C _____ 4 + 4

12. A _____ 8 + 0

    B _____ 0 + 3

    C _____ 6 + 0

Challenge: Look at number 12. Without finding the sums, how can you tell which combination is the largest?

_____

_____

Mastering Math Facts: Addition and Subtraction © 2009 Richard S. Piccirilli, Scholastic Teaching Resources

Name _____ Date _____

Find the Triplets

Directions: Draw a ring around the names and number combinations that are triplets—they all have the same answers. There are 10 triplets. Find them all!

Example

Bettina	2 + 2	Rob	3 + 5	Lou	4 + 6
Becca	1 + 4	Robby	4 + 4	Lucy	8 + 2
Bertha	0 + 4	Roberta	7 + 1	Lucia	2 + 9

1.

Sally	7 + 3
Sarah	4 + 6
Sandy	5 + 3

2.

Jan	6 + 3
Joe	4 + 5
John	8 + 1

3.

Bill	6 + 7
Will	5 + 8
Phil	4 + 7

4.

Tom	6 + 7
Tim	4 + 9
Ted	8 + 5

5.

Ryan	5 + 5
Raul	7 + 3
Ron	2 + 8

6.

Ben	4 + 7
Len	6 + 6
Van	8 + 4

7.

Kay	9 + 7
Kate	8 + 8
Kathy	7 + 9

8.

Ray	8 + 6
Rae	7 + 7
Raja	5 + 9

9.

Maria	7 + 7
Meg	9 + 5
Mair	6 + 9

10.

Patti	9 + 2
Pemba	7 + 4
Paola	3 + 8

11.

Wanda	8 + 5
Winnie	4 + 8
Winston	6 + 6

12.

Cady	4 + 3
Carla	5 + 2
Carolyn	1 + 6

13.

Tito	9 + 6
Ito	7 + 8
Veto	6 + 9

14.

Hilda	8 + 7
Tilda	9 + 6
Gilda	6 + 9

15.

Alexa	5 + 3
Alec	2 + 6
Alexis	4 + 4

Name _____ Date _____

Valuable Words

Directions: Can you find the words that are most valuable? Look at the key. Each letter has a number assigned to it. Find the value of each word below by adding up the value of each letter.

········· **Examples** ··········

1. dad = $\dfrac{5 + 1 + 5}{} = \underline{11}$

2. bad = $\dfrac{9 + 1 + 5}{} = \underline{15}$

Key

a	b	d	e	i
1	9	5	2	3

3. add = _____ = ____

4. dead = _____ = ____

5. be = _____ = ____

6. id = _____ = ____

7. did = _____ = ____

8. Dee = _____ = ____

9. idea = _____ = ____

10. Deb = _____ = ____

11. dab = _____ = ____

12. Ed = _____ = ____

Put a ★ next to the most valuable word and circle the least valuable word.

Mastering Math Facts: Addition and Subtraction © 2009 Richard S. Piccirilli, Scholastic Teaching Resources

Name _____   Date _____

Breaking Up Is Easy

Directions: Break up each fact into a new combination with three or four addends. There are many different ways this can be done!

Example

$9 + 8 = 17$ $\underline{6} + \underline{3} + 8 = 17$ (three addends)

$9 + \underline{4} + \underline{4} = 17$ (three addends)

$\underline{3} + \underline{3} + \underline{3} + 8 = 17$ (four addends)

$\underline{6} + \underline{3} + \underline{3} + \underline{5} = 17$ (four addends)

Number Fact	Number Fact as Three Addends	Number Fact as Four Addends
1. $6 + 7 = 13$	___ + ___ + ___ = 13	___ + ___ + ___ + ___ = 13
2. $9 + 7 = 16$	___ + ___ + ___ = 16	___ + ___ + ___ + ___ = 16
3. $8 + 5 = 13$	___ + ___ + ___ = 13	___ + ___ + ___ + ___ = 13
4. $7 + 4 = 11$	___ + ___ + ___ = 11	___ + ___ + ___ + ___ = 11

Challenge: Write each of the following sums as three addends: 12, 14, and 15.

$12 =$ ___ + ___ + ___

$14 =$ ___ + ___ + ___

$15 =$ ___ + ___ + ___

Name _____ Date _____

Number Facts in Disguise
Part 1

Directions: Below are number facts in disguise. One of the number facts has been broken up and disguised. For example: 5 + 2 + 3 is also 7 + 3 or (5 + 2) + 3. The 7 was disguised as 5 + 2!

Find the sum of each of the disguised number facts. But first, remember to put parentheses around the first two numbers.

········· **Example** ·········

1. $(5 + 2) + 3 =$ __10__

2. 2 + 4 + 8 = ____

3. 2 + 5 + 6 = ____

4. 4 + 4 + 4 = ____

5. 3 + 4 + 7 = ____

6. 4 + 4 + 8 = ____

7. 6 + 3 + 7 = ____

8. 2 + 5 + 8 = ____

9. 3 + 2 + 6 = ____

10. 3 + 4 + 4 = ____

11. 6 + 2 + 1 = ____

12. 5 + 4 + 3 = ____

Mastering Math Facts: Addition and Subtraction © 2009 Richard S. Piccirilli, Scholastic Teaching Resources

Name _____ Date _____

Number Facts in Disguise
Part 2

Directions: Uncover the addition facts that are in disguise. Find the sum of the numbers in parentheses and then find the sum of the total problem.

∙∙∙∙∙∙∙∙∙∙ **Example** ∙∙∙∙∙∙∙∙∙∙

1. $5 + (5 + 2) =$ _?_____

   $5 +$ __7__ $=$ __12__

2. $(6 + 1) + 6 =$ _?_____

   ____ $+ 6 =$ ____

3. $4 + (3 + 5) =$ _?_____

   $4 +$ ____ $=$ ____

4. $(4 + 3) + 6 =$ _?_____

   ____ $+ 6 =$ ____

5. $(1 + 1 + 5) + 8 =$ _?_____

   ____ $+ 8 =$ ____

6. $(3 + 4) + (3 + 2) =$ _?_____

   ____ $+$ ____ $=$ ____

7. $(3 + 3) + (3 + 5) =$ _?_____

   ____ $+$ ____ $=$ ____

8. $(3 + 3) + 8 =$ _?_____

   ____ $+ 8 =$ ____

9. $(4 + 2 + 2) + 4 =$ _?_____

   ____ $+ 4 =$ ____

10. $(3 + 4) + 7 =$ _?_____

    ____ $+ 7 =$ ____

Working With Addition Relationships

ACTIVITY 1   What's My Number?

Two players each select a number card from a facedown pile, but may not look at their own card. At the same time, they hold their own card on their forehead for their partner to see. You (or a classmate) then give the sum of the two addends and each player determines his or her own number. The first player to say his or her number wins a point.

MATERIALS
Student Response Cards
(page 160)

· ·

ACTIVITY 2   Skip, Hop, and Jump to Number Facts

When students need more practice with certain number facts, try the Hop, Skip, and Jump technique. Start with a number fact for which the first addend is the Hop (have a student hop to that number). The second addend is the Skip (have the student skip forward on the number line, "adding" the number of spaces. The Jump, then, is the sum of the Hop and the Skip.

MATERIALS
Large number line on the board or on the floor (can be marked with painter's tape, which is easy to remove)

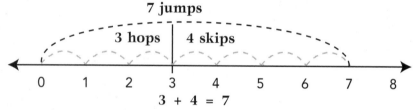

$$3 + 4 = 7$$

· ·

ACTIVITY 3   Tell Me a Story

Build flexible thinking by having students rename numbers. Put the cards in a pile. Explain that Aces count as 1, Jacks count as 11, Queens count as 12, and Kings count as 13. A volunteer chooses a card. The volunteer writes a story for the card in four number sentences. For example, if a student picks a 9 card from the deck, then the story could be:

MATERIALS
Deck of playing cards

$$5 + 4 = 9$$
$$2 + 2 + 2 + 2 + 1 = 9$$
$$4 + 4 + 1 = 9$$
$$2 + 2 + 2 + 3 = 9$$

Variation: After the story is told, another volunteer goes to the board to continue the story by writing another number sentence. Other volunteers continue in the same manner.

Name _____ Date _____

Follow the Rules

Directions: The number at the top of each box tells you an adding rule. Follow the rule for every number in the box and fill in the answers.

Add	5
3	8
9	14
7	
5	
8	

Add	9
3	
7	
6	
8	
4	

Add	1
8	
2	
7	
6	
4	

Add	7
9	
6	
8	
5	
4	

Add	2
7	
6	
4	
8	
9	

Add	4
6	
7	
5	
9	
8	

Add	6
6	
4	
9	
7	
8	

Add	3
6	
8	
5	
9	
7	

Add	8
3	
7	
4	
5	
8	

Name _____ Date _____

Numbers Are Shaping Up

Directions: Make number facts with shapes as clues. Fill in each shape with a one-digit number. The two numbers you use must add up to the sum you see listed. When two different shapes are used, choose two different numbers. When the two shapes are alike, then use the same number.

Examples

$\boxed{4} + \boxed{3} = 7 \qquad \boxed{4} + \boxed{4} = 8$

1. $\bigcirc + \triangle = 11$

2. $\triangledown + \bigcirc = 11$

3. $\triangle + \triangledown = 11$

4. $\bigcirc + \bigcirc = 11$

5. $\bigcirc + \bigcirc = 12$

6. $\bigcirc + \diamond = 12$

7. $\square + \triangledown = 12$

8. $\bigcirc + \diamond = 12$

9. $\triangleleft + \star = 13$

10. $\square + \star = 13$

11. $\diamond + \bigcirc = 13$

12. $\triangle + \triangle = 14$

Mastering Math Facts: Addition and Subtraction © 2009 Richard S. Piccirilli, Scholastic Teaching Resources

Name _____ Date _____

Fill the Holes

Directions: Find the holes in each chart. Write in the number that completes each addition fact.

Example

Addend	4	7	6	7	8		7	7
Addend	2	3		5		4	6	
Sum	6		12		16	12		11

Addend	9	5			9	5	7	4
Addend	6		4	8		6		5
Sum		13	13	17	18		16	

Addend			7	7	3	7		3
Addend	4	4					3	
Sum	10	12	10	15	12	14	9	8

Addend			9	4	0	2		
Addend	6	2		7		7	3	0
Sum	14	9	14		9		8	6

Mastering Math Facts: Addition and Subtraction © 2009 Richard S. Piccirilli, Scholastic Teaching Resources

Name _____ Date _____

The Function Machine

Directions: Make the Function Machine work by filling in the empty circles with the correct numbers that are missing. You'll see an **IN** number, an **INSIDE** number, and their sum, the **OUT** number.

Example 1

6 / IN / 3 INSIDE / OUT ⑨

Example 2

7 / IN / ⑤ INSIDE / OUT 12

Example 3

⑧ / IN / 8 INSIDE / OUT 16

A.

4 / IN / 2 INSIDE / OUT ◯

○ / IN / 5 INSIDE / OUT 13

6 / IN / ◯ INSIDE / OUT 14

B.

◯ / IN / 7 INSIDE / OUT 14

7 / IN / ◯ INSIDE / OUT 10

9 / IN / ◯ INSIDE / OUT 15

C.

0 / IN / 6 INSIDE / OUT ◯

8 / IN / 7 INSIDE / OUT ◯

3 / IN / ◯ INSIDE / OUT 11

D.

◯ / IN / 9 INSIDE / OUT 14

◯ / IN / 6 INSIDE / OUT 13

6 / IN / ◯ INSIDE / OUT 10

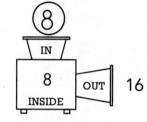
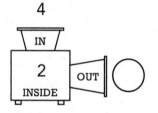
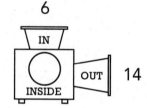
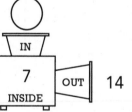
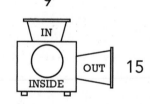
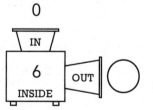
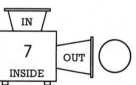
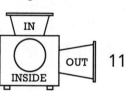
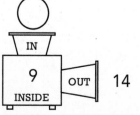
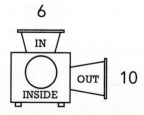

Mastering Math Facts: Addition and Subtraction © 2009 Richard S. Piccirilli, Scholastic Teaching Resources

Tools for Memorizing Facts

Triangular Flash Cards and the Addition-Subtraction Table are flexible tools for addition practice with the entire class, a small group, or individual students.

ACTIVITY 1   Triangular Flash Cards

Cut out the triangles along the cut lines. On the front of each card, write a number fact with the combination numbers in each corner. Leave the apex blank. On the back, do the same, and write the sum at the apex.

MATERIALS
Triangular Flash Card template (page 157) copied and glued to stiff paper to make sets of flash cards.

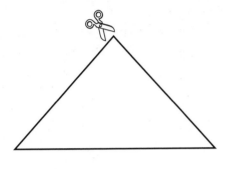

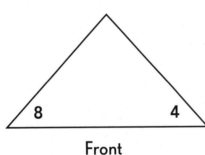

Front

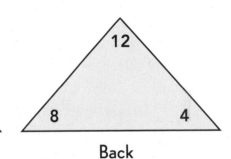

Back

Use the cards in the following activities:

- Show the front of the card, and have students say the missing sum.

- Show the back of the card and with your thumb, cover one of the corner numbers for students to identify the hidden addend.

- Have students sort the cards by tables. Students can group cards by the 1s table, the 2s table, the 3s table, and so on. This will help students to begin recognizing the three numbers that go together to make up a number fact. Once the number "family" is gathered, students can put the cards in order. For example, for the 3s table, students would use this order: 3 + 0, 3 + 1, 3 + 2, 3 + 3, 3 + 4 . . . .

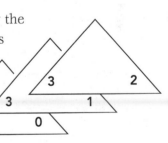

- Have students sort the cards by answers 0–18. For example, all the flash cards with a sum of 6 are placed in one pile, while all flash cards with the sum of 8 are placed in another pile. Each student can concentrate on one sum.

- Have students sort the cards into two groups. One group should include sums that are 10 or less and the other group includes answers that are greater than 10.

- Have students sort the cards by even answers and odd answers.

- Have students pull out the cards that have addends that are both even numbers. Then have students find the cards that have addends that are both odd numbers. Finally have students sort cards with one addend that is odd and the other is even.

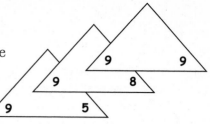

• Sort by strategies. Working with one strategy at a time, have students find all the cards that have facts that support the given strategy. Find all the doubles and Almost-Doubles, Zero the Hero, Speedy 9s, and 10 Again facts. Students can also sort the cards by matching up all the turnarounds.

• Use the cards as a source for randomly selecting combinations for quizzes, as well as for oral practice.

ACTIVITY 2 Working With the Addition-Subtraction Table

On screen, display the Addition-Subtraction Table. For each addition strategy you teach, shade in the sums on one of the charts. Using page 158, students can show and compare six strategies side by side.

MATERIALS
Small Addition-Subtraction Table (page 158) and copy of large table (page 61) for each student

+	0	1	2	3	4	5	6	7	8	9
0	0	1	2	3	4	5	6	7	8	9
1	1	2	3	4	5	6	7	8	9	10
2	2	3	4	5	6	7	8	9	10	11
3	3	4	5	6	7	8	9	10	11	12
4	4	5	6	7	8	9	10	11	12	13
5	5	6	7	8	9	10	11	12	13	14
6	6	7	8	9	10	11	12	13	14	15
7	7	8	9	10	11	12	13	14	15	16
8	8	9	10	11	12	13	14	15	16	17
9	9	10	11	12	13	14	15	16	17	18

Display on screen the Addition-Subtraction Table on page 61. Ask questions, such as:

1. How can you use the chart to do addition?

2. What number appears on the chart 10 times? Why does it appear so many times?

3. What numbers do you see as an answer only once? Why?

4. Why do all the two-digit sums appear in the lower right-hand side of the chart?

5. How does the chart show subtraction?

6. What patterns do you see when you shade in the strategies in the chart?

Name _____ Date _____

Addition-Subtraction Table

Directions: Use this chart to color in addition-fact patterns you've learned and to answer questions about the 100 addition and 100 subtraction facts.

+	0	1	2	3	4	5	6	7	8	9
0	0	1	2	3	4	5	6	7	8	9
1	1	2	3	4	5	6	7	8	9	10
2	2	3	4	5	6	7	8	9	10	11
3	3	4	5	6	7	8	9	10	11	12
4	4	5	6	7	8	9	10	11	12	13
5	5	6	7	8	9	10	11	12	13	14
6	6	7	8	9	10	11	12	13	14	15
7	7	8	9	10	11	12	13	14	15	16
8	8	9	10	11	12	13	14	15	16	17
9	9	10	11	12	13	14	15	16	17	18

Chapter 4

DRILL

STEP 4 Use Meaningful Drill to Master Addition Facts

In the previous chapter, we focused on practice. Now students are ready for drill—repeated practice that helps students commit number facts to memory. The goal here is for facts to become automatic so that students can work quickly and efficiently when adding and apply their skills to more complex mathematics work.

Drill sessions are intended to develop fluency with a skill students already possess. Meaningful drill is possible when students have the necessary prerequisites to attain mastery. The work you've done with students in the first three chapters has equipped them with addition-fact understanding, strategies, and practice in a variety of contexts. With this background, drill should be enjoyable, not stressful; It gives students a chance to show what they know and further build their confidence. On the flip side, drill without prerequisites leads to poor results. Students may not yet be comfortable enough with the meaning of addition or with strategic ways to figure out facts. Drilling them at this point will discourage them and delay mastery.

- What is an effective drill session?

Effective drill sessions use a variety of activities and materials that interest students who are ready to commit the number facts to memory. Drill sessions should be short and done frequently so that students gradually respond faster. Frequent use of practice sheets can be helpful.

Classroom games are included in this chapter to make drills motivating to children. You'll find interactive activities called Captured, Bingo, Show and Tell, and Shout Out. You can play them again and again, even after students have attained mastery. The review will help students maintain their skills.

The most important thing to remember about drill is to be sure students see it as a positive experience. The upcoming Short and Sweet Drills (page 68) is an activity that enables students to see their progress from one drill session to the next. The drills have one focus—recall.

- What's in this chapter?

This chapter includes games, flash cards, reproducibles, and activities that you can use on screen or on the board. Many activities are teacher-directed, while there are also games for small groups or individual students. The goal of each suggestion is making number facts automatic to your students. Some of the games and activities require quick responses. This is a non-intrusive way of introducing a time component. Choose timed activities carefully, especially for students who may be uncomfortable in timed situations.

You set the pace with the drills in the chapter and can follow through with remediation procedures found in Chapter 5.

0s and 9s Drill

This drill promotes "no fatigue" math, using two strategies: Zero the Hero and Speedy 9s.

ACTIVITY   Rattle-Off and Roll

Copy the combinations below on chart paper, the board, or flash cards, or show it on screen. Ask a volunteer to "rattle off" the answers as they "roll" along with each combination. Point to each combination in order or skip around.

9	8	6	0	9	9	0
+ 3	+ 9	+ 0	+ 8	+ 0	+ 7	+ 0

0	2	0	9	3	6	0
+ 1	+ 9	+ 2	+ 5	+ 0	+ 9	+ 4

7	1	0	4	9
+ 0	+ 9	+ 5	+ 9	+ 9

Variation 1: Copy the problems onto paper for students to do written drill.

Variation 2: Using the same idea of rattling off answers, use other combinations that reflect strategy usage. You can do the same kind of quick thinking for the strategies such as Adding 1 More, Adding 2 More, 10 Again, or Almost-Doubles. Keep in mind that it is best to limit the activity to only two strategies at a time.

Naming Facts

This random fact drill helps students work fast on addition combinations.

ACTIVITY Follow Me

Write a plus sign and the chart of numbers listed below on chart paper, the board, or a transparency. Show it to the class.

1. Say: *Follow me.*

2. Point to the 5.

3. Point to the plus sign.

4. Point to the 4.

5. Ask: *What is the answer?* (9) Point to the 9 after students give the correct answer.

6. Continue in this manner with other addition combinations, using the numbers listed on the chart, pointing to the plus sign between each.

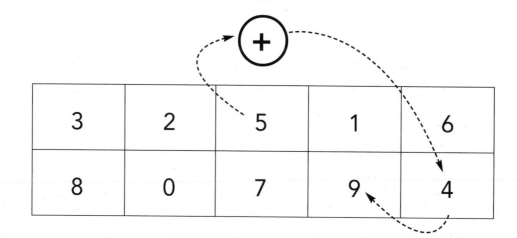

Variation: Invite students, one by one, to lead the Follow Me exercise.

Name _____ Date _____

Combination Roll-Off

Directions: In this drill game you must be the first to roll all the different die combinations! Here are the steps to play:

1. Find a partner and gather a pair of dice with dot stickers with numbers 4–9.

2. Start with two players. Each one rolls a die. The player with the higher roll starts. He or she is Player A. The other partner is Player B.

3. Player A rolls both dice, adds the two numbers shown, and says the sum out loud. Then he or she checks off the answer by marking an X in the box in the Player A column next to that combination.

4. Players take turns rolling. Follow these rules:
   - If the combination has already been marked, the player marks nothing and the next player goes.
   - If doubles are rolled, the player gets another turn. BUT If two 4s are rolled, the player loses a turn.

5. The first player with all the boxes marked in his or her column is the winner.

		PLAYER A	PLAYER B
9	5 4	☐	☐
10	5 5	☐	☐
	6 4	☐	☐
11	6 5	☐	☐
	7 4	☐	☐
12	6 6	☐	☐
	7 5	☐	☐
	8 4	☐	☐
	9 3	☐	☐

		PLAYER A	PLAYER B
13	4 9	☐	☐
	5 8	☐	☐
	6 7	☐	☐
14	7 7	☐	☐
	8 6	☐	☐
	9 5	☐	☐
15	6 9	☐	☐
	7 8	☐	☐
16	8 8	☐	☐
17	8 9	☐	☐
18	9 9	☐	☐

Sum Drills

These drills encourage students to recall number-combination facts by focusing on the sums.

ACTIVITY 1   Who's Related?

Write the combinations listed below on the board, chart paper, or on screen. Explain to students that most of the combinations in each row are related by the same sum. However, there are visitors with different answers mixed in. Point out that their goal is to find the visitors.

Have students scan the problems to figure out the common sum. Then have them determine which combinations don't have that sum. Call on volunteers to name the combinations that aren't in the family and to circle them. In each row, children should find at least two visitors. (*1. common sum = 13, visitors are Andrew and Anna; 2. common sum = 14, visitors are Beth and Bella; 3. common sum = 10, visitors are Carlos, Connie, and Corey*)

1.

5	6	4	6	7	8	9
+ 8	+ 7	+ 9	+ 8	+ 6	+ 5	+ 6
Adam	Alice	Ava	Andrew	Antonio	Ashley	Anna

2.

8	5	7	6	7	5	9
+ 6	+ 9	+ 6	+ 8	+ 7	+ 9	+ 2
Ben	Bart	Beth	Brian	Brandon	Bo	Bella

3.

9	4	7	5	2	1	5
+ 2	+ 6	+ 3	+ 8	+ 8	+ 9	+ 7
Carlos	Cara	Clem	Connie	Cindy	Caleb	Corey

ACTIVITY 2   Matchmaker, Matchmaker

Have 10 students line up at the front of the room. Five students will have a number combination in front of them. Another five students will hold the matching answer cards. One student plays Matchmaker. The Matchmaker must match the student with the combination and the student holding the correct answer card.

MATERIALS

Flash cards with combinations and separate answer cards with the sums on them

ACTIVITY 3   Let's Make An Arrangement

Display a set of five preselected flash cards. Ask a student to rearrange them. The student should arrange the flash cards by answers from least to greatest.

MATERIALS
Set of flash cards

Example:

Random order

| 7
+ 2 | 5
+ 7 | 9
+ 4 | 4
+ 3 | 2
+ 8 |

Arranged in order

| 4
+ 3 | 7
+ 2 | 2
+ 8 | 5
+ 7 | 9
+ 4 |

ACTIVITY 4   Slap the Card

Take out five preselected flash cards at a time. One should have a sum that is larger than the other four. Lay the flash cards on a table in front of a pair of students. Tell students that the object is to be the first player to identify the card with the largest sum. The winner is the first player to slap the card when you say "Go!" The winner gets to keep the card. Then you'll turn over five more preselected flash cards. If you wish to keep score, set a time limit and have the players count up the cards when they've finished.

MATERIALS
Set of flash cards

| 8
+ 0 | 3
+ 7 | 4
+ 7 | 4
+ 5 | 4
+ 4 |

Variation: Change the object of the game to be to slap the flash card that has the smallest sum or has a specific answer. For example, you say might say, "12" and the two students have to quickly find which combination adds to 12.

Short and Sweet Drills

When students have had sufficient practice at addition facts and can recall many automatically, it is a good time to introduce these drills. Students should feel comfortable and view the experience in a positive light.

ACTIVITY   Make a Drill Booklet

Have students make a booklet for doing their drills. (See the next page for directions.) Students should label the first booklet Addition Drills, and they can later create one called Subtraction Drills. They should number each page 1–10.

For each drill session, you will call out or show students 10 facts. They must write the answer only in their booklet. (Note: to keep the drills quick, students should not copy the entire fact.) You can generate sets of 10 addition facts by doing the following:

MATERIALS
Booklet Instructions (page 69), 11- by 14-inch copy paper, flash cards

- Use the Follow Me activity (page 64) to generate random facts.
- Select facts that the class or group consistently has trouble with.
- Draw combinations from a bag of slips written by students.
- Choose two cards from a deck of playing cards that has tens and face cards removed. Ask students to write the sum of the two cards. (Aces equal 1.)
- Select combinations that test one or more strategies.
- Give facts from a single number family, such as 0s, 5s, 7s, or 9s.
- Have each student submit five number facts to include in the drill. From this collection select 10. Use the collection again for another drill.

Variation 1: For any facts students miss in a drill, have them make personal flash cards.

Variation 2: Record students' progress on a graph.

Variation 3: Have students write and illustrate story problems for a set of facts given in one of the drills.

Variation 4: Allow students to conduct drills with a peer or small group.

Booklet Instructions for Short and Sweet Drills

1 Use a large sheet of paper. Place it horizontally, facedown. Fold the paper in half, top to bottom. Crease and unfold.

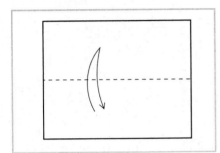

2 Fold in half, left to right. Crease it sharply, and leave it folded.

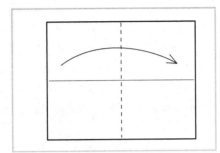

3 Fold again in the same direction. Unfold this last step.

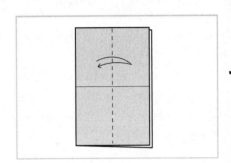

4 Cut in from the left side to the center, following the cut line. Make sure to stop at the middle crease. Open the whole sheet.

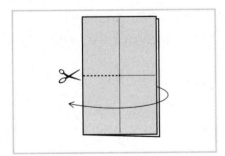

5 Fold in half top to bottom, so that the two long edges meet.

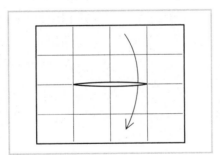

6 Push the two outer edges in, so that the slit opens and the inner pages are formed. Crease the edges of all pages to make the book.

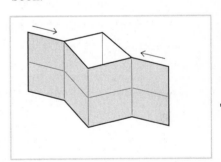

7 Design your book!

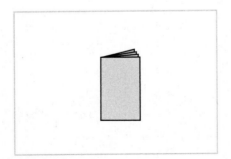

Adapted from *Origami Math*, Grades 2–3 © 2004 by Karen Baicker. Published by Scholastic Inc. Used by permission.

Find-the-Pattern Drill

This drill helps students match the 100 addition combinations with their sums.

ACTIVITY Helping Mr. Summy

Introduce the activity by telling the following story: *One day when Mr. Summy was walking to his classroom, he dropped 100 flash cards with all the addition facts you know. He had worked the night before to get them organized. He wanted to show his class the pattern that he saw when he had his flash cards matched with their sums. Let's find out what the pattern was.*

MATERIALS

Index cards, 100 addition fact flash cards for each student or group

Have each student or group of students make a set of sum cards by writing the numbers 0–18 on a set of 19 index cards. Ask students to spread out the cards in order. Put out the flashcards and have students (individually or in small groups) look at each flash-card combination and find the sum. Then have them place the card under the number that represents the sum. Have students find the pattern that Mr. Summy wanted to show his class. (They write 0–18 on a piece of paper. After each number, they record the number of cards that appeared in each pile.)

Ask: *How many cards are under each sum? Which sum has the most combinations? Which sums have the fewest combinations? What patterns do you see?* (Students should begin to see that the facts are made of addends 0–9 and that the sum with the most combinations of addends 0–9 is 9—the sum right in the middle. This is even clearer when you look at a 100 facts chart.)

Variation 1: For younger students, use combinations with sums of 10 or less.

Variation 2: Have students do the activity independently, solitaire-style.

0	1	2	3	4	5
6	7	8	9	10	11
12	13	14	15	16	17
18					

Game-Like Drills

What better way to have students practice number facts than through a game? Having students make the materials saves preparation time.

· ·

ACTIVITY 1 Facts-Mastery B-I-N-G-O

Ask students to randomly fill in 19 of the 24 spaces with numbers 0–18. Have students fill in the remaining five squares with any numbers that they would like to repeat. (For younger students, the boards can be prepared in advance.) Tell students that they will put a marker on their card when they find the number that is the sum of the flash card you show. A winning card has five marked squares across, down, or diagonally. You may want to give small prizes as rewards for winning cards.

MATERIALS
Bingo Game Board (page 159) copy for each student, markers (counters, coins, buttons, or objects can be used as Bingo markers)

Extension: To create subtraction boards, randomly fill in 10 spaces of the board with 0–9 and then fill in the remaining spaces, repeating these numbers.

Variations: These alternative rules provide more ways to use the Bingo boards students have created.
- Play Four Corners: The first one to fill in each of the four corners must call out, "Four Corners!"
- X-MO: The first to fill in the two diagonal lines, making a large X, must call out, "X-MO!"

· ·

ACTIVITY 2 Around-and-Around Drill

When used early in the year, this activity can serve as a quick informal assessment of the mastery level of each individual or each class.

MATERIALS
We're Going in Circles (page 72), copy for each student

Show page 72 on screen. Ask a student to give you the sum as you point to a number outside the circle. The student then has to add that outside number to the number in the center. Tell them that they should all be ready with an answer for each space and see if they can call out answers without pausing. Once students understand how to fill in the circles, assign the practice page.

Name _____ Date _____

We're Going in Circles

How many addition facts do you know for each number? Add the number in the center of the circle to each number on the outside of the circle. Write each sum on the line given.

　　　　Work as quickly as you can. If you don't know one, leave it blank. Later, go back and fill in the blanks. Remember, these are the facts you need to study!

Example

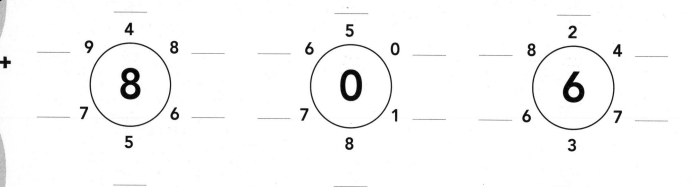

12
9　　　7　　　　7
　　4　　2
13　　**5**　　11
　　8　　6
　　　9
14

Mastering Math Facts: Addition and Subtraction © 2009 Richard S. Piccirilli, Scholastic Teaching Resources

Name _____ Date _____

Hi, Partner!

Directions: Each number below is next to another number. Think of them as partners. Now add the partners together and write your answer below each pair.

.... **Example** ....

2 ⌄ 5   1 ⌄ 8   0 ⌄ 4

__7__ __6__ __9__ __8__ __4__

1. 4 ⌄ 3   5 ⌄ 2   0 ⌄ 6

___ ___ ___ ___ ___

2. 6 ⌄ 5   7 ⌄ 2   8 ⌄ 1

___ ___ ___ ___ ___

3. 5 ⌄ 9   9 ⌄ 4   6 ⌄ 3

___ ___ ___ ___ ___

4. 6 ⌄ 2   7 ⌄ 3   5 ⌄ 8

___ ___ ___ ___ ___

5. 6 ⌄ 5   8 ⌄ 4   7 ⌄ 0

___ ___ ___ ___ ___

Small-Group Drills

These activities can be set up in centers for students to practice during independent work time.

ACTIVITY 1 Shout Out!

Have students gather in pairs or small groups. A dealer turns over two cards from the deck. The first player to shout out the correct sum keeps the two cards. In case of ties, the cards are returned to the deck and are shuffled, and the game continues. The winner is the player who has the most cards at the end of play.

MATERIALS
Deck of playing cards (face cards, 10s, and jokers removed) for each group (Aces equal 1.)

ACTIVITY 2 Winner Takes All

The object of this game is to have a higher sum than your opponent with a given pair of playing cards.

Have partners split a deck of playing cards. Each player turns over two cards from the deck at the same time. Each player says the sum of the cards he or she has turned over. (Jokers and face cards count as zero. Aces equal one.) The player with the higher sum wins both pairs. In case of ties (sums are equal), the cards are returned to the bottom of the deck and the game continues. If a wrong answer is given by either player, all four cards are returned to the bottom of the deck.

MATERIALS
Deck of playing cards for each pair

ACTIVITY 3 Egg-citing Facts

To prepare the activity for pair work in centers, randomly number the bottom of the cups in an egg carton 0–9, and choose two numbers to repeat for the remaining two cups. Demonstrate how to use the tool: Place two markers in the carton, close the top, and scramble them about. Open the carton to find where the markers have landed. Tell students that the numbers on which the markers have landed are the addends. Have students add the two numbers, and them scramble again.

Variation 1: Pairs of students can play. Several egg cartons can be made so that everyone in the classroom can be playing the game at the same time.

Variation 2: Send home the egg carton game with students who need extra practice.

MATERIALS
Empty egg carton, two small markers (dry beans or beads)

74

Whole-Class Drills

ACTIVITY 1   Captured

Group students into two teams and tell them that the object of the
game is for one team to capture the other team. Have each team
lined up against a wall. At the same time, show the first person in
each line a flash card. The first player to respond with the correct sum wins the round for
his or her team. The winning team captures the opposing player, so both winner and loser
go to the end of the winner's line. The game continues in the same manner as the lines
move forward. The team that captures the most players at the end of play (when you call
time, after about 10 minutes) is the winner.

MATERIALS
Addition flash cards

ACTIVITY 2   Show and Tell

Show a flash card or say an addition
expression. Have the class show the
sum by holding up the correct Student
Response Card.

   When appropriate, have students tell what
strategies they might have used.

MATERIALS
Set of Student Response
Cards (page 160) for each
student, addition flash
cards (optional)

Tip: Use the Student Response Card for other drill activities in place of oral answers. It is
sometimes best when requesting answers to give students time to select their response card
and then at the teacher's signal, raise their card. This ensures that students do not depend
on others for answers.

ACTIVITY 3   One-Minute Challenges

Hand out this series of drill exercises one at a time—over the
course of one or two weeks. Each time remind students to do their
best and leave blanks for answers they don't know automatically.
Have them stop at the end of 1 minute and circle and write their
scores (the number they answered correctly) at the bottom of the
page. Ask them to circle any incomplete facts on the page and
study these facts to prepare for the next challenge. Have students keep their One-Minute
challenges in a folder so that you and they can compare their progress from one challenge
to the next.

MATERIALS
Copy of Addition One-
Minute Challenge drills
(pages 76-80) for each
student

Name _____ Date _____

Addition One-Minute Challenge #1

Directions: In one minute, complete as many combinations as you can. At first, you may not be able to do them all. Do your best and try to improve your score for the next challenge.

Hint: If you don't know an answer, leave it blank. When you finish, look for the combinations you left blank so you can study them for the next time.

	a	b	c	d	e	f
1.	5 + 3	8 + 0	1 + 2	0 + 0	2 + 6	7 + 3
2.	8 + 9	5 + 8	9 + 6	4 + 9	8 + 8	5 + 9
3.	9 + 9	4 + 7	7 + 9	5 + 7	2 + 4	6 + 9
4.	4 + 6	7 + 5	3 + 8	8 + 6	3 +2	0 + 2
5.	9 + 3	1 + 0	7 + 4	9 + 4	8 + 3	6 + 4

Mastering Math Facts: Addition and Subtraction © 2009 Richard S. Piccirilli, Scholastic Teaching Resources

Number correct
_____
30   Total

Name _____ Date _____

Addition One-Minute Challenge #2

Directions: In one minute, complete as many combinations as you can. At first, you may not be able to do them all. Do your best and try to improve your score for the next challenge.

Hint: If you don't know an answer, leave it blank. When you finish, look for the combinations you left blank so you can study them for the next time.

	a	b	c	d	e	f
1.	6 + 2	4 + 4	7 + 2	5 + 4	3 + 5	6 + 3
2.	5 + 5	6 + 4	3 + 9	8 + 3	6 + 5	0 + 1
3.	8 + 4	3 + 7	1 + 6	7 + 6	9 + 2	4 + 8
4.	0 + 7	6 + 1	7 + 8	5 + 3	2 + 7	1 + 8
5.	1 + 0	5 + 2	3 + 3	2 + 4	4 + 9	7 + 0

Mastering Math Facts: Addition and Subtraction © 2009 Richard S. Piccirilli; Scholastic Teaching Resources

30 / **Number correct**
Total

Name _____ Date _____

Addition One-Minute Challenge #3

Directions: In one minute, complete as many combinations as you can. At the end, compare how you did with Challenges 1 and 2.

Hint: If you don't know an answer, leave it blank. When you finish, look for the combinations you left blank so you can study them for the next time.

	a	b	c	d	e	f
1.	3 + 2	3 + 8	7 + 3	6 + 2	4 + 4	7 + 2
2.	6 + 5	3 + 9	6 + 0	7 + 5	8 + 2	3 + 6
3.	8 + 4	5 + 0	4 + 7	1 + 6	3 + 7	9 + 2
4.	1 + 8	2 + 0	3 + 1	0 + 4	4 + 5	5 + 3
5.	2 + 9	7 + 4	0 + 2	6 + 9	1 + 7	0 + 6

$$\frac{}{30}$$ **Number correct**

Total

Name _____ Date _____

Addition One-Minute Challenge #4

Directions: In one minute, complete as many combinations as you can. At the end, compare how you did with Challenges 1, 2, and 3.

Hint: If you don't know an answer, leave it blank. When you finish, look for the combinations you left blank so you can study them for the next Challenge.

	a	b	c	d	e	f
1.	8 + 2	7 + 0	0 + 3	9 + 1	3 + 6	9 + 2
2.	6 + 2	0 + 4	3 + 1	3 + 9	6 + 8	8 + 7
3.	0 + 1	2 + 2	6 + 6	1 + 3	4 + 1	2 + 0
4.	5 + 5	7 + 7	9 + 8	5 + 9	4 + 0	2 + 9
5.	2 + 5	5 + 4	9 + 9	7 + 8	1 + 6	0 + 7

$$\frac{}{30}$$ **Number correct**

Total

Name _____ Date _____

Addition One-Minute Challenge #5

Directions: In one minute, complete as many combinations as you can. At the end, compare how you did with Challenges 1, 2, 3, and 4.

Hint: If you don't know an answer, leave it blank. When you finish, look for the combinations you left blank so you can study them.

	a	b	c	d	e	f
1.	2 + 0	3 + 1	0 + 4	2 + 3	1 + 4	4 + 3
2.	6 + 9	0 + 2	7 + 4	0 + 5	6 + 7	2 + 6
3.	7 + 3	0 + 8	3 + 8	6 + 0	7 + 5	8 + 2
4.	7 + 9	7 + 7	8 + 8	9 + 1	9 + 0	5 + 1
5.	9 + 2	7 + 6	1 + 6	8 + 5	6 + 2	4 + 4

$$\frac{\quad\quad}{30} \quad \frac{\text{Number correct}}{\text{Total}}$$

Talk About It: How did you do? Did you improve your score? How much did you improve from Challenge 1 to Challenge 5?

Mastering Math Facts: Addition and Subtraction © 2009 Richard S. Piccirilli, Scholastic Teaching Resources

Name _____ Date _____

Show Off!

Directions: Show all the addition facts that you know! Complete the addition chart by adding the numbers in the left column with the numbers in the top row.

Hint: Give answers to combinations that you know right away. If you don't know a sum without counting, just leave it blank. The blanks will show you what you need to study.

Addition Number Facts

+	5	3	7	0	1	8	4	9	2	6
2	7									
4										
0										
6										
1										
9										
5										
3										
7										
8										

ASSESSMENT AND RETEACHING

STEP 5 Practical Diagnosis and Remediation of Addition and Subtraction Facts

• What's the matter with the traditional timed-test assessment of number facts?

Many teachers give the class a test of all 100 number facts for students to complete independently in 2 to 5 minutes. Usually, there is little or no preparation before the 100 facts are given for a diagnosis. For many students, this can be stressful. They want to do well but are afraid of failure. The time limit also increases tension.

The information gained is of little value for several reasons. First, students may have performed under stress. In addition, there is usually no way to know whether students counted on their fingers, used tally marks, or depended on another aid. The test may also show that some students did only the easy items and left many they knew blank. It's hard to identify strengths and weaknesses with this practice and trying to plan remedial work becomes challenging.

• What's a better way of diagnosing number-facts mastery?

To understand a more constructive approach to diagnosis, imagine the class performing a play. You wouldn't put on a play without first having led numerous rehearsals and a dress rehearsal. The same holds true for diagnosing basic number facts. Basic number facts should be diagnosed when students are ready. Students should be assessed when they understand the process of addition, can use strategies, have gained fluency from practice, and have developed automaticity through drill (see Chapters 1–4).

Students should take a diagnostic test that is teacher directed and places less emphasis on time. The focus is on which facts students have mastered. With the approach described in this chapter, you've got the chance to celebrate students' successes, while uncovering areas they have not yet mastered. This approach decreases test anxiety, creates a positive atmosphere, and is success-oriented since students know in advance what they will be tested on. They will have taken practice tests, and they will look forward to showing what they know.

• What do I need to know about the Diagnostic Test?

The Diagnostic Test (page 93) is identical to the Practice Tests (pages 87–91) you will give students, with all items in a different order. The test procedures are identical. In fact, if you need an additional diagnostic test, you may use one of the practice tests. Keep in mind that the Diagnostic Test is always teacher directed and is a test for which students have prepared.

• When should the Diagnostic Test be given?

The Diagnostic Test is given once the prerequisites of meaning, strategies, practice, and drill have been met and Practice Tests have been given. When most students know the majority of the number facts, as demonstrated by their Practice Tests, then you're ready to use the Diagnostic Test. This chapter covers procedures for both Addition and Subtraction diagnosis. The Subtraction Practice and Diagnostic Tests are included in Chapter 10.

• How are the Practice Tests and the Diagnostic Test administered?

Directions appear on page 85. They are identical for both types of tests.

• What is the best way to score them?

Have students correct the tests as you read the answers. Students should circle items they missed. Students track their progress on a Progress Sheet (page 92) for Practice Test results and on the Addition Facts Summary Sheet (page 94) for the Diagnostic Test result.

• How do I use the student Summary Sheet?

Have students fill in the Addition Facts Summary Sheet with stars or smiley faces for each item they answered correctly on the Diagnostic Test. Have them leave blank examples they missed. Students now have a record of what they know and what they need to work on. Once you know a student's weaknesses, you have the basis for remedial work. If a student misses a significant number of facts give a retest after remedial work is complete. Be sure to recognize students for what they have attained.

• How do I remediate number-fact weaknesses?

Following the five-step sequence presented in this addition section of this book should leave you with very few students who need reteaching. After the Diagnostic Test has been corrected and the Summary Sheet has been completed, identify each student's strengths, as well as which number facts they still need to master. First, determine if errors were results of carelessness. In this case, little may need to be done. Next, look for error patterns, which may indicate a need to relearn a specific strategy.

For example, see if there are many errors in one number family. Did the student not use Zero the Hero, Speedy 9s, or another strategy you taught? Use your judgment in determining causes and what to do about them. Here are some suggestions for reteaching:

1. Interview the student to find out whether he or she is using a strategy. For troublesome facts, use the technique in Mastering Troublesome Facts (page 95).

2. Consider more practice and/or drill that can be done with activities or reproducibles, as suggested in the activities at the end of this chapter and in Chapters 2–4.

3. Have students make flash cards for the missed facts. They can play games at home or with a peer. As time permits, meet with students to evaluate their progress.

• What's in this chapter?

Included are materials and directions for conducting Practice Tests and the Diagnostic Test. You'll also find student progress and summary sheets and additional remediation activities to ensure that all students achieve addition-fact mastery.

Successful Mastery:
A Guide to Using the Addition and Subtraction
Practice Tests and the Diagnostic Tests

The suggestions below help you and your students get the maximum benefits from using the tests found in this chapter and in Chapter 10.

1. You lead the Practice and Diagnostic Tests. These tests are effective only if they are teacher directed. Set a positive tone when you administer the tests. Let students understand that the purposes is to help them master their number facts and boost their math confidence.

2. Use the tests only after students are ready. You determine when there is some level of mastery, as demonstrated on the Practice Tests, before the formal Diagnostic Test is given.

3. Explain to students that the Practice Tests are the same as the Diagnostic Test. Point out that the Diagnostic Test will contain the same basic number facts, just in a different order. This should help to relieve some stress and test-taking anxiety. Let students know ahead of time what the Diagnostic Test will look like.

4. Use Practice Tests frequently. They are short and are teacher-student corrected to immediately identify student strengths and areas that need work. How many Practice Tests you use depends on your students' needs. The more you provide, the more opportunity there is for students to improve their weaknesses. With continued practice, students should become more successful as they prepare for the Diagnostic Test.

5. Don't forget about advanced students. For the advanced math student, use at least one Practice Test and Diagnostic Test so that both you and the student have evidence of number-fact mastery. Advanced math students should continue to engage in math activities, including math investigations, reports, individual or team projects, and constructing physical math models. While you work with other students on mastering facts, you can provide them with engaging math puzzles and brain teasers, and you may also want to give them a role in helping their peers.

A Script for Conducting Practice Diagnostic Tests For Addition and Subtraction

The following is a script for you to adapt as you administer a Practice or Diagnostic Test. Before you begin, hand out to each student a copy of the selected test placing it facedown. Direct students to keep their tests turned over and to wait for a signal to begin.

Maintain a calm, supportive, and positive tone for these assessments. It is imperative that students do not see them as stressful. Remind students to leave out facts that they are unsure of and that this is not the time for counting, tallying, or using other aids.

- To set the ground rules:

Say: *This is a Practice Test (or Diagnostic Test).*

We have been working on our basic addition (or subtraction) number facts for several days. You will now have the chance to show what you've learned and also to show what you may still need to work on.

This is what will happen when I give you the signal to turn your test sheet over. You will see 100 number facts. We will all work together on them in this way. I will read each one to you and then you will write the answer. It is very important that you work only on the problem that I am reading. The reason for this is that it will keep the right pace for everyone. I will give you time to write the answer to each number fact.

Remember, we're trying to find those basic number facts that you absolutely know and those you are either unsure of or don't know. Do not guess at answers. If you do not know it, leave it blank. The blank problems will show us which number facts we need to work on more.

Is everyone ready? (Wait for students to indicate they are ready.) *Good, now remember, if you know the answer, write it down. If you are unsure of the answer or don't know it, then do not write any answer.*

- To begin the test:

Say: *Please turn your test sheet over. Let's begin! Stay with me and respond only to the number fact that I read to you.*

Note: Read each of the number facts from the form that you are using.

Be sure to walk around the classroom to observe if students are working on the same combination that is being read.

Periodically, remind students to answer only if they are sure of the fact.

Suggestions for Administering the Test

• Timing

Determine a reasonable response time. Generally, the first time students do this activity, you might consider pausing several seconds in between answers. When students have more experience with this format, cut down on the time intervals between examples. An effective timing device and visual cue is to touch your thumb to your pinky and then touch each of your next three fingers. This will be a consistent visual cue, as well.

• Correcting

When you have completed the Practice or Diagnostic Test, correct the papers immediately. Use the following suggestions.

1. Read each example with the answer. Students will correct their own papers using a different colored pencil or marker as they follow along with you. Have them fill in the correct answers where there are incorrect answers or blanks.

2. Have students record their progress at the bottom of the test sheet and on the Progress Sheet graph on page 92. After they correct the Diagnostic Test, have them complete the Addition Diagnostic Summary Sheet on page 94.

3. Have students make flash cards for the number facts that they still need to practice.

4. Assess individual progress as well as the class progress by checking over each student's results. Also, you'll want to assign remedial activities, such as flash-card activities, games, and, in some cases, a review of specific strategies. See page 83, 95, and 96 for suggestions for remediation.

5. Celebrate successes with bulletin-board displays, badges, certificates of mastery, notes to parents, notes on report cards, and announcements at parent-teacher conferences.

Name _____   Date _____

Addition Practice Test #1

	a	b	c	d	e	f	g	h	i	j
1.	0 + 9	5 + 7	1 + 2	7 + 5	2 + 6	9 + 4	6 + 0	3 + 8	8 + 1	4 + 3
2.	5 + 9	1 + 7	7 + 2	2 + 5	9 + 6	6 + 4	8 + 8	3 + 0	4 + 1	0 + 3
3.	1 + 9	7 + 7	2 + 2	9 + 5	6 + 6	3 + 4	8 + 0	4 + 8	0 + 1	5 + 3
4.	7 + 9	2 + 7	9 + 2	6 + 5	3 + 6	8 + 4	4 + 0	0 + 8	5 + 1	1 + 3
5.	2 + 9	9 + 7	6 + 2	3 + 5	8 + 6	4 + 4	0 + 0	5 + 8	1 + 1	7 + 3
6.	9 + 9	6 + 7	3 + 2	8 + 5	4 + 6	0 + 4	1 + 8	5 + 0	7 + 1	2 + 3
7.	6 + 9	3 + 7	8 + 2	4 + 5	0 + 6	5 + 4	1 + 0	7 + 8	2 + 1	9 + 3
8.	3 + 9	8 + 7	4 + 2	0 + 5	5 + 6	1 + 4	7 + 0	2 + 8	9 + 1	6 + 3
9.	8 + 9	4 + 7	0 + 2	5 + 5	1 + 6	7 + 4	9 + 8	2 + 0	6 + 1	3 + 3
10.	4 + 9	0 + 7	5 + 2	1 + 5	7 + 6	2 + 4	9 + 0	6 + 8	3 + 1	8 + 3

Number correct
_____
100   Total

Name _____ Date _____

Addition Practice Test #2

	a	b	c	d	e
1.	5 + 5 = _____	8 + 9 = _____	9 + 5 = _____	0 + 6 = _____	3 + 2 = _____
2.	1 + 2 = _____	7 + 7 = _____	3 + 4 = _____	8 + 5 = _____	1 + 8 = _____
3.	6 + 1 = _____	5 + 8 = _____	9 + 0 = _____	1 + 6 = _____	0 + 1 = _____
4.	8 + 8 = _____	9 + 8 = _____	4 + 4 = _____	5 + 0 = _____	2 + 4 = _____
5.	5 + 9 = _____	6 + 2 = _____	0 + 0 = _____	3 + 7 = _____	4 + 9 = _____
6.	0 + 3 = _____	2 + 1 = _____	2 + 5 = _____	9 + 7 = _____	0 + 9 = _____
7.	7 + 4 = _____	0 + 5 = _____	3 + 3 = _____	1 + 5 = _____	2 + 3 = _____
8.	9 + 6 = _____	1 + 7 = _____	5 + 3 = _____	9 + 4 = _____	0 + 8 = _____
9.	3 + 5 = _____	4 + 2 = _____	7 + 5 = _____	3 + 0 = _____	2 + 7 = _____
10.	2 + 8 = _____	0 + 7 = _____	9 + 3 = _____	6 + 5 = _____	1 + 9 = _____
11.	1 + 4 = _____	8 + 7 = _____	7 + 6 = _____	7 + 9 = _____	8 + 2 = _____
12.	2 + 0 = _____	9 + 2 = _____	8 + 4 = _____	2 + 9 = _____	6 + 4 = _____
13.	5 + 7 = _____	6 + 8 = _____	1 + 0 = _____	6 + 6 = _____	4 + 0 = _____
14.	1 + 1 = _____	0 + 4 = _____	2 + 2 = _____	5 + 2 = _____	7 + 2 = _____
15.	8 + 6 = _____	0 + 2 = _____	2 + 6 = _____	5 + 1 = _____	1 + 3 = _____
16.	3 + 6 = _____	8 + 3 = _____	7 + 8 = _____	3 + 1 = _____	6 + 3 = _____
17.	5 + 6 = _____	9 + 9 = _____	4 + 5 = _____	7 + 1 = _____	6 + 7 = _____
18.	4 + 7 = _____	8 + 1 = _____	4 + 6 = _____	6 + 9 = _____	4 + 3 = _____
19.	6 + 0 = _____	3 + 9 = _____	3 + 8 = _____	7 + 0 = _____	9 + 1 = _____
20.	7 + 3 = _____	4 + 1 = _____	8 + 0 = _____	5 + 4 = _____	4 + 8 = _____

Number correct
_____
100   Total

Mastering Math Facts: Addition and Subtraction © 2009 Richard S. Piccirilli, Scholastic Teaching Resources

Name _____ Date _____

Addition Practice Test #3

	a	b	c	d	e	f	g	h	i	j
1.	6 + 2	4 + 4	7 + 2	5 + 4	0 + 0	3 + 5	6 + 3	3 + 8	0 + 8	7 + 3
2.	5 + 5	6 + 4	3 + 9	8 + 3	6 + 5	0 + 1	3 + 6	8 + 2	7 + 5	6 + 0
3.	8 + 4	3 + 7	1 + 6	7 + 6	9 + 2	4 + 8	4 + 6	9 + 3	4 + 7	5 + 0
4.	0 + 3	5 + 8	9 + 4	5 + 7	2 + 1	9 + 5	5 + 6	1 + 5	5 + 9	9 + 8
5.	7 + 7	7 + 9	8 + 8	6 + 6	8 + 7	1 + 2	9 + 6	9 + 9	8 + 6	1 + 9
6.	9 + 1	2 + 5	1 + 1	3 + 4	3 + 0	1 + 3	8 + 0	8 + 1	0 + 9	8 + 9
7.	9 + 0	5 + 1	3 + 2	4 + 0	2 + 2	7 + 1	6 + 8	2 + 6	6 + 7	0 + 5
8.	8 + 5	4 + 1	2 + 8	9 + 7	0 + 6	1 + 7	2 + 9	7 + 4	0 + 2	6 + 9
9.	1 + 0	5 + 2	3 + 3	2 + 4	4 + 9	7 + 0	4 + 2	4 + 3	1 + 4	2 + 3
10.	0 + 7	6 + 1	7 + 8	5 + 3	2 + 7	1 + 8	4 + 5	0 + 4	3 + 1	2 + 0

Mastering Math Facts: Addition and Subtraction © 2009 Richard S. Piccirilli, Scholastic Teaching Resources

Number correct

$\dfrac{\quad\quad}{100}$ Total

Name _____ Date _____

Addition Practice Test #4

	a	b	c	d	e	f	g	h	i	j
1.	3 + 5	3 + 8	7 + 3	6 + 2	4 + 4	7 + 2	5 + 4	0 + 0	6 + 3	0 + 8
2.	6 + 5	3 + 9	6 + 0	7 + 5	8 + 2	3 + 6	0 + 1	8 + 3	6 + 4	5 + 5
3.	8 + 4	5 + 0	4 + 7	1 + 6	3 + 7	9 + 2	7 + 6	4 + 8	4 + 6	9 + 3
4.	2 + 1	9 + 8	9 + 5	5 + 6	1 + 5	0 + 3	5 + 8	9 + 4	5 + 7	5 + 9
5.	1 + 2	7 + 7	7 + 9	8 + 8	6 + 6	8 + 7	9 + 6	9 + 9	8 + 6	1 + 9
6.	9 + 1	8 + 9	0 + 9	2 + 5	1 + 1	3 + 4	3 + 0	1 + 3	8 + 0	8 + 1
7.	7 + 1	6 + 8	2 + 6	0 + 5	6 + 7	9 + 0	5 + 1	3 + 2	4 + 0	2 + 2
8.	2 + 9	7 + 4	0 + 2	6 + 9	1 + 7	0 + 6	9 + 7	2 + 8	4 + 1	8 + 5
9.	1 + 0	5 + 2	3 + 3	2 + 3	1 + 4	4 + 3	7 + 0	4 + 2	4 + 9	2 + 4
10.	1 + 8	2 + 0	3 + 1	0 + 4	4 + 5	5 + 3	2 + 7	0 + 7	6 + 1	7 + 8

Mastering Math Facts: Addition and Subtraction © 2009 Richard S. Piccirilli, Scholastic Teaching Resources

Number correct

_____

100   Total

Name _____ Date _____

Addition Practice Test #5

	a	b	c	d	e
1.	1 + 5 = ____	2 + 2 = ____	0 + 5 = ____	2 + 7 = ____	8 + 5 = ____
2.	8 + 1 = ____	0 + 0 = ____	4 + 0 = ____	9 + 5 = ____	8 + 3 = ____
3.	8 + 7 = ____	5 + 6 = ____	3 + 6 = ____	8 + 4 = ____	5 + 2 = ____
4.	1 + 2 = ____	3 + 9 = ____	9 + 2 = ____	6 + 5 = ____	0 + 3 = ____
5.	5 + 0 = ____	2 + 3 = ____	0 + 7 = ____	5 + 3 = ____	5 + 8 = ____
6.	4 + 1 = ____	2 + 6 = ____	0 + 4 = ____	8 + 8 = ____	2 + 1 = ____
7.	3 + 7 = ____	3 + 3 = ____	9 + 4 = ____	2 + 8 = ____	8 + 9 = ____
8.	6 + 0 = ____	3 + 8 = ____	5 + 7 = ____	9 + 9 = ____	7 + 2 = ____
9.	9 + 8 = ____	5 + 1 = ____	4 + 9 = ____	4 + 3 = ____	6 + 3 = ____
10.	0 + 8 = ____	0 + 2 = ____	6 + 6 = ____	8 + 6 = ____	4 + 7 = ____
11.	0 + 9 = ____	6 + 9 = ____	6 + 4 = ____	7 + 0 = ____	9 + 1 = ____
12.	6 + 7 = ____	1 + 8 = ____	0 + 6 = ____	6 + 1 = ____	1 + 9 = ____
13.	4 + 2 = ____	2 + 5 = ____	6 + 2 = ____	1 + 6 = ____	1 + 1 = ____
14.	1 + 3 = ____	0 + 1 = ____	7 + 9 = ____	3 + 1 = ____	9 + 7 = ____
15.	9 + 0 = ____	2 + 4 = ____	5 + 9 = ____	7 + 4 = ____	2 + 0 = ____
16.	1 + 0 = ____	9 + 3 = ____	4 + 8 = ____	7 + 3 = ____	7 + 7 = ____
17.	5 + 5 = ____	7 + 1 = ____	3 + 2 = ____	6 + 8 = ____	5 + 4 = ____
18.	9 + 6 = ____	7 + 5 = ____	3 + 4 = ____	4 + 6 = ____	7 + 6 = ____
19.	8 + 0 = ____	1 + 7 = ____	3 + 5 = ____	1 + 4 = ____	2 + 9 = ____
20.	7 + 8 = ____	8 + 2 = ____	4 + 4 = ____	3 + 0 = ____	4 + 5 = ____

Number correct

$\dfrac{}{100}$ Total

Name _____ Date _____

Progress Sheet for Number-Fact Practice Tests

Directions: Use colored pencils, markers, or crayons to record your progress after you complete each Practice Test.

SCORE
Number Correct

#1	#2	#3	#4	#5

Mastering Math Facts: Addition and Subtraction © 2009 Richard S. Piccirilli, Scholastic Teaching Resources

Name _____ Date _____

Addition Diagnostic Test

	a	b	c	d	e	f	g	h	i	j
1.	5 +3	8 +0	1 +2	0 +0	2 +6	7 +3	0 +9	3 +5	6 +1	4 +2
2.	9 +0	5 +2	3 +0	2 +7	5 +1	2 +5	3 +3	1 +1	7 +1	7 +2
3.	1 +7	4 +5	0 +6	1 +9	0 +8	1 +4	1 +8	5 +4	0 +7	3 +4
4.	6 +0	8 +1	4 +3	2 +3	5 +0	1 +6	4 +4	2 +1	8 +5	0 +5
5.	8 +2	7 +0	0 +3	9 +1	3 +6	9 +2	6 +3	1 +5	2 +0	4 +1
6.	6 +2	0 +4	3 +1	3 +9	6 +8	8 +7	1 +3	6 +6	2 +2	0 +1
7.	9 +3	1 +0	7 +4	9 +4	8 +3	6 +4	7 +6	8 +4	6 +5	3 +7
8.	4 +6	7 +5	3 +8	8 +6	3 +2	0 +2	7 +8	5 +6	9 +7	4 +8
9.	9 +9	4 +7	7 +9	5 +7	2 +4	6 +9	9 +5	6 +7	2 +9	4 +0
10.	8 +9	5 +8	9 +6	2 +8	4 +9	8 +8	5 +9	9 +8	7 +7	5 +5

Number correct
----
100   Total

Name _____ Date _____

Addition Diagnostic Summary Sheet

Directions: Use your Diagnostic Test to show what you know! Draw a ☺ or ☆ for all the number facts that you answered correctly. For each fact you didn't answer correctly, leave it blank. These are the facts you'll need to study!

Addition Facts I Know!

+	0	1	2	3	4	5	6	7	8	9
0										
1										
2										
3										
4										
5										
6										
7										
8										
9										

Number correct _____

Mastering Math Facts: Addition and Subtraction © 2009 Richard S. Piccirilli, Scholastic Teaching Resources

Mastering Troublesome Facts

ACTIVITY 1 Back to Basics

For reteaching materials, go back to Chapters 2 to 4 to find the appropriate activities or reproducibles to meet the needs of your students who have not yet mastered specific facts or fact tables.

ACTIVITY 2 Multisensory Recall

Have students follow this procedure for each troublesome fact:

1. See and Say: Look at the flash card that has the answer on it and say it. For example, say "Three plus four equals seven."

2. Cover up the entire flash card.

3. Write the fact from memory.

4. Compare what you wrote to the fact shown on the flash card.

5. If you wrote the fact correctly, move on to the next card and repeat steps 1–4. If not, make corrections to match the flash card and repeat steps 1–4 with the same flash card until you can do it from memory.

MATERIALS

Paper, pencil, flash cards for the troublesome facts

ACTIVITY 3 Reteaching Flash Cards

Have students create and take home the facts they need to work on. Or keep the set on hand for volunteers and aides and peers to review with students. Set a time frame for students to study and learn these facts. Do several quick checks along the way to assess students' progress.

MATERIALS

3- by 5-inch index cards, cut in half (each makes two 3- by 2½-inch flash cards) or Triangular Flash Cards (see page 157).

ACTIVITY 4   Writing and Drawing Number-Fact Problems

Have students write a story problem using a difficult number fact.
Then have them illustrate the number fact. For example:
If the difficult number fact is 6 + 7 = 13, the story problem
may be:

MATERIALS
Booklets for Short and
Sweet Drills (see pages 68
and 69)

*For Mrs. Brown's class baseball team, we chose 6 boys and 7 girls.
How many students from Mr. Brown's class were chosen for the
baseball team?*

The illustration might consist of six boys and seven girls dressed in baseball uniforms or
with bats, baseballs, and mitts.

ACTIVITY 5   Beat the Facts

Encourage students to put their troublesome facts to music. For example, say the following
with a rhythm and beat.

6 + 7 are not mean. That is why they met the queen. 6 + 7 is 13.

8 + 3 climbed Mount Nevin. They thought that they were up in heaven. 8 + 3 is 11.

5 + 8 met a mean queen who was not keen on green. 5 + 8 is 13.

4 + 5 like to dine on grapes from the vine. 4 + 5 is 9.

7 + 8 know that Jean likes to clean. 7 + 8 is 15.

Celebrating Mastery

A key to helping students feel great about their early achievement in math is to recognize their mastery of the 100 addition facts

ACTIVITY Join the All-Stars!

Use the results of the Diagnostic Test to determine who should be recognized for mastering all of their addition facts. The level of accuracy for the 100 facts is up to you. You may consider scores from 90 to 100 percent to qualify for membership as an All-Star. Add each student's name to a celebratory board when he or she has demonstrated mastery.

MATERIALS
Bulletin-board space, colorful paper and borders, flash cards

★ ★ ★ ★ ★ ★ ★ ★ ★

$\begin{array}{r} 7 \\ +\ 4 \\ \hline 11 \end{array}$

NUMBER FACT ALL-STARS

Masters of the 100 Addition Facts

Carol	Alec	Kim
Carlo	Brian T.	Ali
Lily B.	Ziggy	Donnie
Rosa	Sheila	Roberto
Hanna	Amber	Marie
Brooks	Juan	Lizzy
Dan	Tameka	Lynn
Vera	Richard	Rebecca

$\begin{array}{r} 0 \\ +\ 8 \\ \hline 8 \end{array}$

$\begin{array}{r} 6 \\ +\ 7 \\ \hline \end{array}$

$\begin{array}{r} 9 \\ +\ 6 \\ \hline \end{array}$

$\begin{array}{r} 1 \\ +\ 7 \\ \hline 8 \end{array}$

$\begin{array}{r} 8 \\ +\ 5 \\ \hline \end{array}$

Introduction to Subtraction

Subtraction and addition are closely related—subtraction undoes addition. Mastering the 100 subtraction facts has its foundation in mastering the 100 addition facts. The better students know their addition facts, the quicker and easier it is for them to master their subtraction facts. For this reason, the section on subtraction is shorter than the section on addition. If you find that students are struggling with their subtraction facts, it is likely that you may need to assess their mastery of addition facts and reteach as needed (see Chapter 5).

The road to mastering the 100 subtraction facts follows the same five sequential steps outlined in the addition section. They are as follows:

- Teach the meaning of number facts.
- Teach strategies.
- Provide practice.
- Provide meaningful drill.
- Assess and reteach.

- What do I need to know about subtraction?

    1. There are 100 basic subtraction facts.

    2. Addition facts lead to subtraction facts.

    3. Subtraction is checked by addition.

    4. There are three situations in which subtraction is used:

      a. To find what is left

      b. To find how much more is needed

      c. To make comparisons

    5. Subtraction is not commutative as addition is. For example, $3 + 4 = 7$ and $4 + 3 = 7$. In subtraction, $5 - 3 = 2$ but $3 - 5 \neq 2$.

    6. The terms for the numbers used in subtraction are:

$$
\begin{array}{rl}
8 & \text{(minuend)} \\
-\ 3 & \text{(subtrahend)} \\
\hline
5 & \text{(remainder or difference)}
\end{array}
$$

Chapter 6

MAKING MEANING

STEP 1   Teach the Meaning of Subtraction Facts

Students need to understand what subtraction is about: how it relates to addition, how the numbers behave when you subtract, and how it helps to solve problems in their lives. As you guide them, students will understand the value of using subtraction and rise to the challenge of mastering their number facts.

- **How should subtraction facts be taught?**

Subtraction has its foundation in addition. The transition into subtraction should emphasize a natural progression from the knowledge and skill students learned about addition into subtraction. As you teach students how subtraction is related to addition, begin with examples that show missing addends, such as 3 + ? = 7. In this way, you are teaching them to think about subtraction in the context of addition.

Learning subtraction becomes meaningful for students when they use manipulatives. Manipulating counters, colored rods, base-ten rods, number lines, and other materials suggested in the examples in this chapter, provides a concrete and visual understanding of subtraction—the foundation for comprehending the different aspects of the subtraction operation. You'll also want to introduce students to the labels for the numbers in a subtraction fact. Teach students to use the terms minuend, subtrahend, and remainder or difference. Talk about how the terms relate to the addends and sum in addition.

6	(minuend)	2 (addend)
− 4	(subtrahend)	+ 4 (addend)
2	(remainder or difference)	6 (sum)

- **What's in this chapter?**

In this chapter, students learn practical ways to use subtraction through problem solving. They learn how to reason out answers using manipulatives. Students are asked to write their own story problems to further reinforce what subtraction means.

A number of activities in this chapter use concrete materials to demonstrate meaning. You'll also find a reproducible that helps students see the connection between subtraction and addition (page 102), and another that helps to clarify what is meant by finding the difference (page 103).

At the end of the chapter, you'll find suggestions for making posters that emphasize the parts of a subtraction problem and support their understanding of subtraction. Keep in mind that teaching and consistently using the correct terms noted above will help reinforce their learning and avoid confusion as you practice number facts with children.

Name _____ Date _____

Subtraction Story Problems

Directions: Here are some story problems for you to solve. Use counters, the number line, or drawings. Write your answers on the lines.

1. Reid had 8 stamps in his collection. Now he has 12 stamps because his grandmother gave him some more. How many stamps did Reid's grandmother give him?

   _____ stamps

2. In a long-jump contest, Jack's sister, Marty, jumped 10 feet. This was 4 feet farther than Jack's jump. How far did Jack jump?

   _____ feet

3. Zelda has 13 rare birds as pets. She gave 4 of them to her cousin Ethan. How many rare birds does Zelda have left?

   _____ birds

4. Caroline had to call 9 friends to invite them to her birthday party. Her mother made 4 phone calls to help. How many phone calls did Caroline make?

   _____ calls

5. There were 15 commercials on when Daniel watched TV last night. There were 8 commercials about cars. How many commercials were not about cars?

   _____ commercials

6. Ruth is 8 years younger than her 17-year-old sister, Ronda. How old is Ruth?

   _____ years old

7. Geraldo found some money in his pants pocket. He also found 6 cents in his jacket pocket. Now he has 14 cents. How much money was in his pants pocket?

   _____ cents

8. Iva and Irma are sisters who like to run. One day, Iva ran 6 fewer miles than Irma, who ran 11 miles. How many miles did Iva run?

   _____ miles

Mastering Math Facts: Addition and Subtraction © 2009 Richard S. Piccirilli, Scholastic Teaching Resources

Name _____ Date _____

Writing Story Problems for Subtraction Facts

Directions: For each subtraction fact below, write a funny story problem. Remember to end with a question.

Example

For 12 – 3 = 9, you could write: Twelve ants were marching in a band. The director said that 3 had to be drummers. How many ants were not drummers?

1. 10 – 8 = 2 _____

_____

_____

2. 14 – 8 = 6 _____

_____

_____

3. 12 – 4 = 8 _____

_____

_____

4. 9 – 0 = 9 _____

_____

_____

Directions: On the back of this sheet, draw a picture to show one of the story problems you wrote.

Name _____ Date _____

Fill in the Missing Minuend

Directions: Complete each subtraction number fact. Use addition to fill in the missing minuend. For number 1, think: 2 + 7 = 9.

Example

1.
$\dfrac{⑨}{\underset{2}{-\ 7}}$ $\dfrac{\bigcirc}{\underset{5}{-\ 5}}$ $\dfrac{\bigcirc}{\underset{2}{-\ 8}}$ $\dfrac{\bigcirc}{\underset{0}{-\ 9}}$ $\dfrac{\bigcirc}{\underset{5}{-\ 3}}$ $\dfrac{\bigcirc}{\underset{7}{-\ 8}}$

2.
$\dfrac{\bigcirc}{\underset{2}{-\ 9}}$ $\dfrac{\bigcirc}{\underset{4}{-\ 8}}$ $\dfrac{\bigcirc}{\underset{6}{-\ 9}}$ $\dfrac{\bigcirc}{\underset{6}{-\ 7}}$ $\dfrac{\bigcirc}{\underset{7}{-\ 4}}$ $\dfrac{\bigcirc}{\underset{5}{-\ 9}}$

3.
$\dfrac{\bigcirc}{\underset{4}{-\ 7}}$ $\dfrac{\bigcirc}{\underset{3}{-\ 5}}$ $\dfrac{\bigcirc}{\underset{8}{-\ 4}}$ $\dfrac{\bigcirc}{\underset{4}{-\ 9}}$ $\dfrac{\bigcirc}{\underset{1}{-\ 2}}$ $\dfrac{\bigcirc}{\underset{6}{-\ 8}}$

4.
$\dfrac{\bigcirc}{\underset{9}{-\ 5}}$ $\dfrac{\bigcirc}{\underset{0}{-\ 8}}$ $\dfrac{\bigcirc}{\underset{1}{-\ 9}}$ $\dfrac{\bigcirc}{\underset{8}{-\ 7}}$ $\dfrac{\bigcirc}{\underset{2}{-\ 2}}$ $\dfrac{\bigcirc}{\underset{3}{-\ 8}}$

5.
$\dfrac{\bigcirc}{\underset{5}{-\ 8}}$ $\dfrac{\bigcirc}{\underset{5}{-\ 7}}$ $\dfrac{\bigcirc}{\underset{7}{-\ 9}}$ $\dfrac{\bigcirc}{\underset{1}{-\ 8}}$ $\dfrac{\bigcirc}{\underset{9}{-\ 1}}$ $\dfrac{\bigcirc}{\underset{3}{-\ 7}}$

6.
$\dfrac{\bigcirc}{\underset{8}{-\ 9}}$ $\dfrac{\bigcirc}{\underset{9}{-\ 7}}$ $\dfrac{\bigcirc}{\underset{3}{-\ 9}}$ $\dfrac{\bigcirc}{\underset{8}{-\ 3}}$ $\dfrac{\bigcirc}{\underset{8}{-\ 0}}$ $\dfrac{\bigcirc}{\underset{7}{-\ 7}}$

Mastering Math Facts: Addition and Subtraction © 2009 Richard S. Piccirilli, Scholastic Teaching Resources

Name _____   Date _____

Taller Towers

Directions: Compare two towers at a time. Use subtraction to figure out how much taller one tower is than the other. Write the answer on the line.

Example

1.   7   5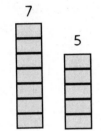

_2_

2.   8   5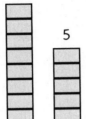

_____

3.   10   6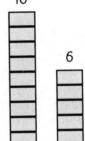

_____

4.   11   7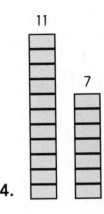

_____

5.   12   5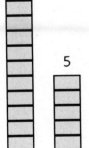

_____

6.   14   8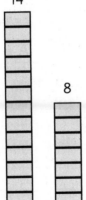

_____

7.   12   5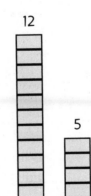

_____

8.   15   8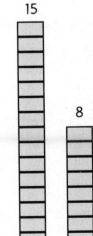

_____

Mastering Math Facts: Addition and Subtraction © 2009 Richard S. Piccirilli, Scholastic Teaching Resources

Demonstrating Subtraction Facts

These activities help to make subtraction facts concrete by using hands-on models.

ACTIVITY 1 — Number-Line Model

Choose interesting subtraction problems to demonstrate on the number line. Relate subtraction to addition, as well, to point out both operations. Begin with the example below.

Example: Between the school library and Ava's classroom there are 12 computers. In her classroom, Ava counted 4 computers. How many computers are in the library?

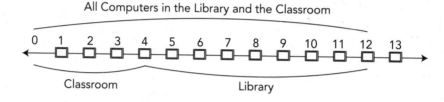

All Computers in the Library and the Classroom

Classroom   Library

ACTIVITY 2 — Subtraction Cut-Up

Use drawings on the board or on chart paper to demonstrate the idea of cutting off a piece of board. Show how you can find out either how much was cut off or how much was left. Also show how big the board was at the start. Write a number sentence for each. Explain the concept that subtraction is finding the missing addend. Model the following samples.

Example A: How much of the board is cut off?

8 + ? = 12

12 – ? = 8

12 – 8 = ?

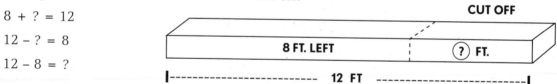

Example B: How much of the board is left?

? + 4 = 12

12 – ? = 4

12 – 4 = ?

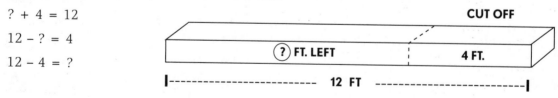

Example C: How long is the board?

8 + 4 = 12

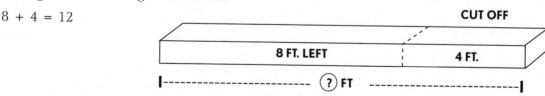

Discuss the thinking behind these problems. Ask: *If you know the amount that was cut off the board and how much is left, how do you find out how long was the board at the start?*

Developing Insights

These activities use discussion and visual models to help students better comprehend the facets of subtraction, including number sense, usage, value, and characteristics.

· ·

ACTIVITY 1   Questions to Build Students' Understanding of Subtraction

Use any of the following questions to prompt discussion.

1. What is subtraction? How is subtraction related to addition?

2. When you have the problem 10 – 8, is it easier for you to think *8 + (what) = 10* or to think *10 take away 8 is 2?*

3. How could you subtract 12 – 7 on a calculator if the minus key is broken?

4. Do you get an even number or an odd number when you subtract
   - an even number from an even number?
   - an odd number from an odd number?

5. In the problem 5 – 3 = 2, which number is the minuend? Which is the subtrahend? Which number do we call the remainder or difference?

6. Explain how to use the labels "addend" and "sum" for the problem 8 – 2 = 6.

7. What would you do if you didn't know the answer to 17 – 9?

8. When you're not at school, where do you use subtraction?

9. In 8 – 5 = 3, what happens when you add the same amount to the minuend and subtrahend?

· ·

ACTIVITY 2   Using Scales and Rods to Model Subtraction Principles

Model how story problems can be solved with balance scales or rods. Explain that you need to balance the scales or show rods that are equal in length.

MATERIALS

Balance scale, marbles or other objects to weigh, or Cuisenaire® rods

Example: Baby Daisy weighs 10 pounds. When she was born a month ago, she weighed 8 pounds. How much weight did she gain in a month?

10

8

The Parts of a Subtraction Number Sentence

Students should learn the parts of a subtraction number sentence, or equation, early on in your instruction. Give students practice reading and writing number sentences. Use posters to reinforce the addend-addend-sum relationship and to name the parts of a subtraction problem.

. . . .

ACTIVITY 1 Writing and Reading Number Sentences

Use the story problems on pages 100 and 116 as a basis for writing and reading equations, also known as number sentences. Make sure that students understand how the number sentence reflects what needs to be done to solve the story problem. Use "x" or "?" for the unknown. Focus, also, on reading the number sentences.

Example: Reid had 8 stamps in his collection. After his grandmother gave him some more he had 12. How many stamps did Reid's grandmother give him?

$$A. (12 = 8 + ?) \text{ or } B. (8 + ? = 12) \text{ or } C. (? + 8 = 12)$$

Read the equations as: A. *Twelve equals eight plus what?* B. *Eight plus what equals twelve?* C. *What plus eight equals twelve?*

Variation: Have students use counting up and down to solve some problems.

. . . .

ACTIVITY 2 Subtraction Posters

Use the following examples as models for posters you can hang in your classroom.

MATERIALS
Posterboard, colored magic markers

$$\begin{array}{r} 8 \ (\text{Sum}) \\ - 5 \ (\text{Addend}) \\ \hline 3 \ (\text{Addend}) \end{array}$$

$$\begin{array}{r} 8 \ (\text{Minuend}) \\ - 5 \ (\text{Subtrahend}) \\ \hline 3 \ (\text{Remainder or Difference}) \end{array}$$

When do we subtract?

We subtract when we want to:

① Find what's left:

Jenelle had 12 cents but lost 7 cents. How much money does she have left?

② Find how much more is needed:

A gumball costs 10 cents. Alberto has 8 cents. How much more money does he need?

③ Make comparisons:

Kiki is 5 feet tall. Her three-year-old little sister is 2 feet tall. How much taller is Kiki than her little sister?

Chapter 7

STRATEGIES

STEP 2 Teach Strategies to Make Learning Subtraction Facts Easier

- What are strategies for subtraction?

Explain to students that they can use strategies to learn subtraction just as they did with addition. They can use patterns, learn tricks, and find shortcuts to learning facts.

The strategies for this chapter include

- Taking Away All of It (subtracting a number from itself)
- Zero the Hero (subtracting 0)
- Go Back One (subtracting 1)
- Speedy 9s (subtracting 9)
- Making Easier Numbers (using 10 to make subtraction easier)
- Think Addition! (thinking of subtraction facts as addition facts with missing addends)

- What are the benefits of using strategies for subtraction?

Students who use strategies master their subtraction facts in less time, with little fatigue, and with reduced anxiety. It's important to continue showing students that you value strategy use in subtraction-fact instruction as they progress through practice and drill (Chapters 8 and 9).

- What are some suggestions for teaching strategies with subtraction?

Let students discover for themselves which strategies help them learn specific subtraction combinations. Students often find it easier to think of $13 - 8 = ?$ as $8 + ? = 13$, for example.

The more emphasis you place on using strategies, the more students will use and value strategies as they practice subtraction facts and find value in them. Learning the strategies by name, participating in classroom discussions about the strategies, writing about the strategies, and referring to class posters that highlight the strategies increase the possibility that students will use strategies more frequently.

> Perhaps the most important subtraction strategy is to think of the corresponding addition fact for a subtraction combination.

- What's in this chapter?

The chapter contains activities that use engaging models and concrete materials to explain what the strategies are and why they work the way they do. You'll find both teacher-led activities and student-centered reproducibles to give your class opportunities to reinforce how the subtraction strategies are used.

The chapter ends with suggestions for making classroom posters (page 114). The posters can serve as a focal point for discussions on strategies. As a reference tool, students can easily refer to them for help as they continue to internalize the strategies.

Making Easy Numbers and Speedy 9s

With this activity, you demonstrate how to adapt problems to use easier numbers when subtracting so that the answer does not change.

ACTIVITY   Show How to Make Easy Numbers

To start, give two subtraction combination, such as 7 – 2 = 5 and 8 – 3 = 5. Demonstrate that when you add a number to the minuend and add the same number to the subtrahend, the answer doesn't change. Inform students that this is called the compensation principle.

MATERIALS
Base-ten blocks or Cuisenaire® rods

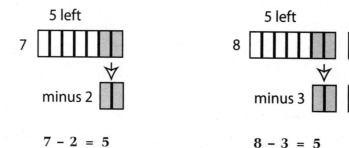

Give a second example. Write 12 – 8 = 4 and 14 – 10 = 4 on the board. Use the rods to show that adding 2 to both the minuend and subtrahend doesn't change the answer. It makes subtracting with 10 easy. You can call this Making Easy Numbers.

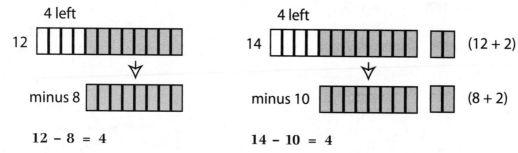

After demonstrating the two examples above, review the Speedy 9s strategy (page 26). Then show two ways to solve 15 – 9.

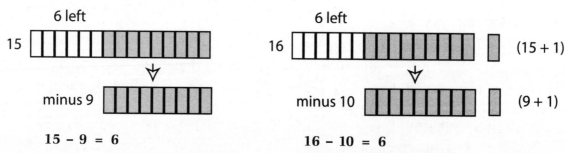

When 9 is subtracted from a number, the number in the answer is 1 more than the number in the ones place of the minuend.

Adding 1 to both the minuend and subtrahend does not change the answer.

Name _____ Date _____

Subtracting With Zero the Hero

Directions: Follow the directions to answer each item.

1. Subtract 0 from each number below.

$$
\begin{array}{cccccccc}
9 & 2 & 1 & 7 & 6 & 8 & 0 & 3 \\
-\,0 & -\,0 & -\,0 & -\,0 & -\,0 & -\,0 & -\,0 & -\,0 \\
\hline
\end{array}
$$

2. What do you notice about the answers?

_____

3. Write a story problem for one of the above subtraction examples.

_____

_____

_____

4. Solve the problems below.

$$
\begin{array}{cccccccc}
3 & 5 & 1 & 7 & 2 & 6 & 0 & 9 \\
-\,3 & -\,5 & -\,1 & -\,7 & -\,2 & -\,6 & -\,0 & -\,9 \\
\hline
\end{array}
$$

5. You can see that the minuend and subtrahend are the same in each of the above problems. What happens when you find the difference of each?

_____

6. Write a story problem for one of the subtraction examples in item 4.

_____

_____

_____

Mastering Math Facts: Addition and Subtraction © 2009 Richard S. Piccirilli, Scholastic Teaching Resources

Name _____ Date _____

Go Back One!

Directions: Subtract 1 from each number below. Write the answer on the line in front of the number.

___ 6   ___ 4   ___ 2   ___ 8   ___ 7   ___ 3   ___ 1   ___ 5   ___ 9

What did you notice when you subtracted 1 from the number?

_____

_____

Speedy 9s for Subtraction

Directions: Here is a strategy that makes subtracting 9 from a number easy. Look at these examples.

1. 1②	2. 1⑦	3. 1④	4. 1⑥	5. 1⑧	6. 1①	7. 1③	8. 1⑤
− 9	− 9	− 9	− 9	− 9	− 9	− 9	− 9
③	⑧	⑤	⑦	⑨	②	④	⑥

For each example above, write the numbers circled in the blanks.

1. _2_ , _3_   2. ____ , ____   3. ____ , ____   4. ____ , ____

5. ____ , ____   6. ____ , ____   7. ____ , ____   8. ____ , ____

9. How can you predict the answer when 9 is the number being subtracted?

_____

_____

10. How is using the Speedy 9s strategy different with subtraction than addition facts?

_____

_____

Mastering Math Facts: Addition and Subtraction © 2009 Richard S. Piccirilli, Scholastic Teaching Resources

Rethinking Subtraction: Make Easy Numbers

These activities demonstrate how to change a subtraction example to make it easier.

- -

ACTIVITY 1 Changing the Combination

1. Write the following problems on the board. Have volunteers provide answers. Discuss with students what they notice about all the answers.

$$\begin{array}{cccccccccc} 5 & & 6 & & 7 & & 8 & & 9 & & 10 & & 11 & & 12 & & 13 \\ -\,1 & & -\,2 & & -\,3 & & -\,4 & & -\,5 & & -\,6 & & -\,7 & & -\,8 & & -\,9 \end{array}$$

2. Explain: As each minuend and subtrahend get larger by the same amount, the answer always stays the same.

3. Give students examples in which the minuend and subtrahend are increased by the same amount. Show students that they can make it easier to subtract by using 10 in the problem.

$$\begin{array}{cccc} 11 & +2 \;\blacktriangleright\; 13 & \quad 15 & +1 \;\blacktriangleright\; 16 & \quad 14 & +4 \;\blacktriangleright\; 18 \\ -\,8 & +2 \;\blacktriangleright\; -10 & \quad -\,9 & +1 \;\blacktriangleright\; -10 & \quad -\,6 & +4 \;\blacktriangleright\; -10 \\ \hline 3 & \qquad 3 & \quad 6 & \qquad 6 & \quad 8 & \qquad 8 \end{array}$$

4. Give students practice. Copy the following examples onto the board with the same blank shapes. Fill in the missing numbers in the circles to make the combinations equivalent, then subtract to fill in the rectangle. The first example shows you how.

$$\begin{array}{ccccc}
12 \;^{+3}\; \textcircled{15} & \quad 15 \;\bigcirc & \quad 17 \;\bigcirc & \quad 11 \quad 16 & \quad 14 \;\bigcirc \\
-\,7 \;^{+3}\; -10 & \quad -\,8 \;-10 & \quad -\,8 \;-10 & \quad -\,5 \;-\bigcirc & \quad -\,9 \;-10 \\
\boxed{5} & \quad \Box & \quad \Box & \quad \Box & \quad \Box
\end{array}$$

- -

ACTIVITY 2 Think Addition!

Think aloud to explain these examples: To subtract 8 from 10 (10 – 8 = ?), think 8 + ? = 10. To subtract 6 from 15 (15 – 6 = ?), think 6 + ? = 15.

Write the following problems on the board. Have students fill in the missing addends.

1. 9 – 5, think 5 + ___ = 9   **4.** 12 – 7, think 7 + ___ = 12   **7.** 8 – 3, think 3 + ___ = 8

2. 7 – 4, think 4 + ___ = 7   **5.** 10 – 5, think 5 + ___ = 10   **8.** 13 – 7, think 7 + ___ = 13

3. 15 – 7, think 7 + ___ = 15   **6.** 9 – 3, think 3 + ___ = 9   **9.** 11 – 9, think 9 + ___ = 11

Name _____ Date _____

Speeding Up Subtraction #1

Directions: You can speed up your work by using patterns when you see subtraction combinations. Try the following strategies to answer the facts correctly:

Zero the Hero: When 0 is subtracted from a number, that number becomes the answer.

$$\begin{array}{r} 2 \\ -\ 0 \\ \hline 2 \end{array}$$ The minuend equals the answer.

Speedy 9s: When 9 is subtracted from a number, the answer is one more than the ones digit in the minuend.

$$\begin{array}{r} 1\,3 \\ -\ 9 \\ \hline 4 \end{array}$$ ← one more than

Hint: There are two examples below that do not follow either strategy.

1.

1	12	6	9	17	8
− 0	− 9	− 0	− 5	− 9	− 0

2.

3	14	0	15	7	18
− 0	− 9	− 0	− 9	− 0	− 9

3.

4	13	5	10	11	2
− 0	− 9	− 0	− 8	− 9	− 0

Challenge: Circle the two problems above that did not work with either Zero the Hero or Speedy 9s.

Mastering Math Facts: Addition and Subtraction © 2009 Richard S. Piccirilli; Scholastic Teaching Resources

Name _____ Date _____

Speeding Up Subtraction #2

Directions: How fast can you recite answers to subtraction combinations? Use these strategies to answer quickly:

Taking Away All of It
When you take the same number away,
you always get 0.

$$\begin{array}{r} 2 \\ -\ 2 \\ \hline 0 \end{array}$$ same ⟵⟶ nothing is left

Making Easy Numbers
Change the number you are subtracting to a 10.
Remember that whatever you add to get a 10,
you have to add that number to the minuend.

$$\begin{array}{rl} 13 & +3 \ \dashrightarrow \ 16 \\ -\ 7 & +3 \ \dashrightarrow \ -10 \\ \hline & \qquad\quad 6 \end{array}$$

1.

$$\begin{array}{r} 11 \\ -\ 8 \\ \hline \end{array} \qquad \begin{array}{r} 6 \\ -\ 6 \\ \hline \end{array} \qquad \begin{array}{r} 14 \\ -\ 8 \\ \hline \end{array} \qquad \begin{array}{r} 15 \\ -\ 8 \\ \hline \end{array} \qquad \begin{array}{r} 9 \\ -\ 9 \\ \hline \end{array} \qquad \begin{array}{r} 15 \\ -\ 7 \\ \hline \end{array}$$

2.

$$\begin{array}{r} 3 \\ -\ 3 \\ \hline \end{array} \qquad \begin{array}{r} 17 \\ -\ 8 \\ \hline \end{array} \qquad \begin{array}{r} 7 \\ -\ 7 \\ \hline \end{array} \qquad \begin{array}{r} 1 \\ -\ 1 \\ \hline \end{array} \qquad \begin{array}{r} 13 \\ -\ 8 \\ \hline \end{array} \qquad \begin{array}{r} 2 \\ -\ 2 \\ \hline \end{array}$$

3.

$$\begin{array}{r} 12 \\ -\ 7 \\ \hline \end{array} \qquad \begin{array}{r} 11 \\ -\ 7 \\ \hline \end{array} \qquad \begin{array}{r} 4 \\ -\ 4 \\ \hline \end{array} \qquad \begin{array}{r} 12 \\ -\ 9 \\ \hline \end{array} \qquad \begin{array}{r} 8 \\ -\ 8 \\ \hline \end{array} \qquad \begin{array}{r} 5 \\ -\ 5 \\ \hline \end{array}$$

Mastering Math Facts: Addition and Subtraction © 2009 Richard S. Piccirilli, Scholastic Teaching Resources

Subtraction Posters

Promote strategies by making posters that you prominently display to remind students of subtraction strategies. Have students reflect on the strategies they use.

ACTIVITY 1   Promote Strategies With Posters

Each time you introduce a new strategy, display a poster of it. Hang the posters on a bulletin board, and let them serve as a reminder that strategies are always available, especially when students have forgotten a subtraction number fact. Use the strategy names listed here or have the class come up with their own names.

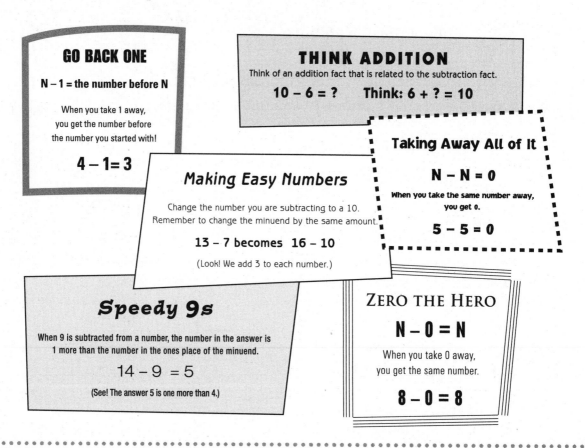

ACTIVITY 2   What Strategy Did You Use?

Give various subtraction combinations, such as the ones below. Ask students to tell what strategy they used or if they didn't use one. Use the above posters for review. There can be more than one strategy for some combinations.

16 – 9	14 – 8	15 – 7	6 – 6	9 – 1	9 – 6
12 – 9	8 – 0	17 – 9	8 – 8	5 – 1	8 – 3

Chapter 8

PRACTICE

STEP 3 Practice Subtraction Facts

The purpose for practicing subtraction facts is for students to repeatedly solve the 100 subtraction facts in different contexts. Students are asked to compare facts, see relationships between them, examine patterns and nuances, and apply strategies. Students must use thinking skills when they practice.

To illustrate, in comparing two number facts such as 10 – 8 and 10 – 7, it is important to help students notice the similarities between the combinations. The example suggests that taking away a larger number from the same minuend means that there is a smaller difference. You can also explain that in the second combination, you are taking away one less and therefore, your answer should be one more than it is in the first combination. With subtraction practice, students will notice these kinds of relationships on their own.

• What are some guidelines for practice?

An important guideline is to have frequent, short, and enjoyable sessions, only after students are aware of meaning and strategies.

• What's in this chapter?

The chapter begins with problem solving to give students an understanding of how subtraction can be experienced in different real-life situations. Next, instruction focuses on how subtraction is related to addition.

Then you will find several reproducibles that require students to compare subtraction facts. The chapter ends with activities that highlight key understandings about subtraction fact answers: all the answers for the basic facts range from 0–9 and specific patterns occur among answers that are odd and even numbers.

Name _____ Date _____

Using Subtraction Facts to Solve Problems

Directions: Solve the problems below. Write your answer on the line and the fact you used in the circle.

FACT

1. John Robinson and Jennifer Wu are friends. How many more letters are in John's full name than Jennifer's? _____ letters

FACT

2. After two days, Ricardo read 13 pages of his favorite book. On Tuesday, he read 7 pages. How many did he read on Monday? _____ pages

FACT

3. Francesca needs 9 cents more in order to buy a 17-cent eraser. How much more money does she have now? _____ cents

FACT

4. Oscar is 16 years old. Ozzie, his younger brother, is 7 years old. How much older is Oscar than Ozzie? _____ years

FACT

5. Newton is 2 feet shorter than his older sister, Velma, who is 5 feet tall. How tall is Newton? _____ feet

FACT

6. When Casey left for school, he had 12 cents in his pocket. When he arrived at school, he only had a nickel. How much money did Casey lose? _____ cents

Mastering Math Facts: Addition and Subtraction © 2009 Richard S. Piccirilli, Scholastic Teaching Resources

Name _____ Date _____

Plug-Ins

Directions: In each item below one of the numbers is left out. Plug in the missing number to complete the problem.

What's in the Pot?

· **Example** · · · · · · · · · · · · · · · · · ·

1. 5 pieces of chicken: 3 are legs, __2__ are wings.

· ·

2. 15 pieces of meat: _____ are meatballs, 9 are sausages.

3. A dozen pieces of vegetables: _____ are carrots, 7 are tomatoes.

4. 8 cups of liquid: 2 cups of milk, _____ cups of water.

5. 11 peppers: _____ are green, 8 are yellow.

How Much Change Do You Get?

1. You had $10 and spent $6. Your change is _____ .

2. You had $5 and spent $4. Your change is _____ .

3. You had $8 and spent $6. Your change is _____ .

4. You had $10 and spent $6. Your change is _____ .

5. You had $5 and spent $2. Your change is _____ .

How Many Are Girls?

1. 14 students are in a room. 7 are boys. _____ are girls.

2. 8 of the 12 students are boys. _____ are girls.

3. Of the 17 people in the room, 9 are boys. _____ are girls.

4. 18 kids are in a room. The number of boys as girls are equal. _____ are girls.

5. 5 of the 14 students in after–school class are boys. _____ are girls.

Subtraction With Concrete Learning and Critical Thinking

Use these activities to further students' understanding of subtraction with practice that is tactile and verbal. Demonstrate subtraction combinations through concrete learning. Then have students test guesses about which numbers yield various answers.

ACTIVITY 1   What's in My Other Pocket?

Line up 5–8 students in front of the room. Give each child an amount of change that is 18 cents or less. On the board, record how much money you give to each volunteer. Ask each child to put some of the money into one pocket and the rest into another.

MATERIALS
Several pennies, nickels, and dimes

Have the first student take the money out of one pocket and tell the amount to the class. Call on a student in the audience to tell the class what is hidden in the volunteer's other pocket. Proceed until you've uncovered the hidden amounts in every volunteer's pocket. As students solve the problems, have them record the equations on the board.

Example: *There are 12 pennies in all. Eight are in one pocket. How many are in the other?*

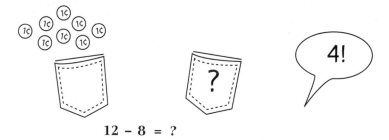

$$12 - 8 = ?$$

ACTIVITY 2   Think About Two Numbers

Display the following numbers.

15   6   13   8   12   9   14

Ask the class to find the two numbers that make a specific answer.

MATERIALS
Board, chart paper, or overhead projector/ interactive whiteboard

Write the list below on the board. For each number, ask:
Are there two numbers from the first set that have a difference of . . . ?

4   5   6   7   8   9   0

Follow the process again. For each number below, ask:
Are there two one-digit numbers from the second set that have a difference of . . . ?

0   1   2   3   4

Name _____ Date _____

A Family of Facts

Directions: In each item below, three numbers can be used to make addition and subtraction facts. Write the family of facts that use the three given numbers.

Example

3, 7, 4

$$3 + 4 = 7$$
$$4 + 3 = 7$$
$$7 - 3 = 4$$
$$7 - 4 = 3$$

1. 6, 8, 14

_____

_____

_____

_____

2. 13, 6, 7

_____

_____

_____

_____

3. 15, 7, 8

_____

_____

_____

_____

4. 9, 8, 17

_____

_____

_____

_____

5. 12, 3, 9

_____

_____

_____

_____

6. 7, 12, 5

_____

_____

_____

_____

7. 4, 13, 9

_____

_____

_____

_____

8. 15, 6, 9

_____

_____

_____

_____

Name _____ Date _____

What's Missing?

Directions: Fill in the box with the missing number to complete the addition fact. Then write the addition fact as a subtraction fact.

1. $3 + \boxed{6} = 9$ $9 - 3 = 6$ **11.** $9 + \boxed{} = 12$ _____

2. $7 + \boxed{} = 9$ _____   **12.** $8 + \boxed{} = 12$ _____

3. $9 + \boxed{} = 9$ _____   **13.** $\boxed{} + 3 = 12$ _____

4. $5 + \boxed{} = 9$ _____   **14.** $\boxed{} + 4 = 12$ _____

5. $2 + \boxed{} = 9$ _____   **15.** $9 + \boxed{} = 11$ _____

6. $0 + \boxed{} = 9$ _____   **16.** $8 + \boxed{} = 11$ _____

7. $4 + \boxed{} = 9$ _____   **17.** $\boxed{} + 8 = 11$ _____

8. $1 + \boxed{} = 9$ _____   **18.** $2 + \boxed{} = 11$ _____

9. $6 + \boxed{} = 12$ _____   **19.** $\boxed{} + 9 = 13$ _____

10. $\boxed{} + 7 = 12$ _____   **20.** $9 + \boxed{} = 13$ _____

Mastering Math Facts: Addition and Subtraction © 2009 Richard S. Piccirilli, Scholastic Teaching Resources

Name _____ Date _____

Which Is Bigger?

Directions: Look at each item. Which subtraction combination has the larger difference? Fill in the circle with an arrow (➡) that points to the larger answer. If the difference of each is the same, fill in the circle with an equal sign (=).

··· **Example** ·································

$8 - 3$ $9 - 5$ because 5 4

1. $7 - 3$ ◯ $9 - 4$ 7. $13 - 6$ ◯ $13 - 7$

2. $5 - 3$ ◯ $10 - 8$ 8. $16 - 8$ ◯ $17 - 8$

3. $9 - 5$ ◯ $2 - 0$ 9. $11 - 7$ ◯ $6 - 1$

4. $8 - 3$ ◯ $5 - 5$ 10. $12 - 3$ ◯ $9 - 9$

5. $10 - 6$ ◯ $12 - 8$ 11. $14 - 9$ ◯ $10 - 3$

6. $12 - 5$ ◯ $14 - 7$ 12. $13 - 4$ ◯ $10 - 1$

Name _____ Date _____

Order, Please!

Directions: Order the following combinations by arranging them from the smallest to the largest difference. See the example below.

Example

12 – 4	___6 – 4 = 2___	smallest difference
8 – 5	___8 – 5 = 3___	
6 – 4	___10 – 4 = 6___	
10 – 4	___12 – 4 = 8___	largest difference

1. 15 – 9 _____
13 – 9 _____
13 – 4 _____
8 – 0 _____

2. 15 – 7 _____
10 – 6 _____
14 – 5 _____
12 – 6 _____

3. 10 – 4 _____
5 – 3 _____
11 – 4 _____
7 – 6 _____

4. 8 – 3 _____
11 – 5 _____
8 – 4 _____
11 – 4 _____

5. 9 – 0 _____
8 – 7 _____
6 – 0 _____
5 – 1 _____

6. 16 – 9 _____
11 – 5 _____
13 – 5 _____
14 – 5 _____

7. 9 – 5 _____
16 – 7 _____
14 – 9 _____
15 – 9 _____

8. 10 – 2 _____
6 – 0 _____
12 – 9 _____
15 – 8 _____

Mastering Math Facts: Addition and Subtraction © 2009 Richard S. Piccirilli, Scholastic Teaching Resources

Name _____ Date _____

Find All the Smallies

Directions: Fill in the answer to each subtraction combination below. Then find the Smallie (the subtraction fact that has the smallest answer for that group). Circle the letter of the Smallie in each group.

1. (M) $10 - 8 =$ __2__
  N $10 - 5 =$ __5__
  D $10 - 6 =$ __4__
  Y $10 - 7 =$ __3__

2. C $9 - 5 =$ ____
  G $8 - 5 =$ ____
  F $7 - 5 =$ ____
  A $6 - 5 =$ ____

3. F $17 - 8 =$ ____
  Q $17 - 9 =$ ____
  W $16 - 8 =$ ____
  T $14 - 7 =$ ____

4. H $15 - 8 =$ ____
  U $12 - 4 =$ ____
  A $9 - 0 =$ ____
  T $15 - 7 =$ ____

5. Z $13 - 7 =$ ____
  T $10 - 4 =$ ____
  S $1 - 0 =$ ____
  E $4 - 2 =$ ____

6. V $18 - 9 =$ ____
  R $10 - 1 =$ ____
  M $5 - 0 =$ ____
  P $14 - 5 =$ ____

7. S $13 - 8 =$ ____
  A $13 - 9 =$ ____
  Y $9 - 0 =$ ____
  Z $14 - 5 =$ ____

8. H $13 - 6 =$ ____
  L $12 - 7 =$ ____
  S $10 - 1 =$ ____
  D $12 - 4 =$ ____

9. Q $5 - 0 =$ ____
  N $8 - 2 =$ ____
  A $7 - 3 =$ ____
  L $10 - 7 =$ ____

10. U $16 - 9 =$ ____
  X $14 - 8 =$ ____
  P $12 - 7 =$ ____
  I $10 - 6 =$ ____

11. R $7 - 2 =$ ____
  G $10 - 6 =$ ____
  E $11 - 8 =$ ____
  C $11 - 3 =$ ____

12. P $10 - 6 =$ ____
  S $10 - 8 =$ ____
  M $10 - 5 =$ ____
  E $10 - 3 =$ ____

Uncover the secret message! Over each number in the code below, write the letter that you circled in the matching problem above.

__M__ ____ ____ ____
  1   2   3   4

____ ____ ____ ____ ____ ____ ____ ____
  5   6   7   8   9   10   11   12

Name _____ Date _____

Who Are the Twins?

Directions: You have found a set of twins when both combinations have the same answer. Circle 10 sets of twins.

Example:

(Jan, Jon) $4 - 2 = 2$ Alex $12 - 5 = 7$ (Ella, Bella) $14 - 6 = 8$
$8 - 6 = 2$ Alec $10 - 4 = 6$ $12 - 4 = 8$

1.
Shameka $12 - 5$
Janeka $14 - 7$

2.
Ed $12 - 7$
Ted $13 - 8$

3.
Keith $14 - 8$
Heath $15 - 7$

4.
Ben $18 - 9$
Len $12 - 3$

5.
Gilbert $7 - 4$
Wilbert $9 - 6$

6.
Jake $8 - 0$
Blake $6 - 0$

7.
Jonah $14 - 7$
Hannah $15 - 8$

8.
Jill $13 - 6$
Will $15 - 8$

9.
Tori $13 - 7$
Laurie $11 - 4$

10.
Kea $13 - 5$
Tia $14 - 9$

11.
Cal $6 - 3$
Nell $11 - 8$

12.
Devon $11 - 7$
Kevin $8 - 4$

13.
Darrell $10 - 5$
Terrell $14 - 9$

14.
Aaron $12 - 6$
Erin $14 - 8$

15.
Guy $9 - 5$
Kai $11 - 5$

Mastering Math Facts: Addition and Subtraction © 2009 Richard S. Piccirilli, Scholastic Teaching Resources

Name _____ Date _____

The Right Location

Directions: Put each of the 27 combinations in the right location—under the correct answer.

Combinations

Examples

1. $14 - 5 = 9$	8. $7 - 4$	15. $10 - 7$	22. $13 - 4$
2. $9 - 5 = 4$	9. $11 - 2$	16. $12 - 6$	23. $16 - 8$
3. $11 - 9$	10. $12 - 5$	17. $9 - 7$	24. $12 - 8$
4. $9 - 8$	11. $8 - 7$	18. $12 - 4$	25. $15 - 8$
5. $10 - 6$	12. $14 - 7$	19. $14 - 8$	26. $11 - 8$
6. $13 - 8$	13. $14 - 9$	20. $9 - 4$	27. $8 - 6$
7. $6 - 5$	14. $13 - 7$	21. $10 - 2$	

Locations

1

1. _____
2. _____
3. _____

2

1. _____
2. _____
3. _____

3

1. _____
2. _____
3. _____

4

1. $9 - 5$
2. _____
3. _____

5

1. _____
2. _____
3. _____

6

1. _____
2. _____
3. _____

7

1. _____
2. _____
3. _____

8

1. _____
2. _____
3. _____

9

1. $14 - 5$
2. _____
3. _____

Name _____ Date _____

Odds and Evens

Directions: Which are oddballs? Find and solve the 10 problems with odd answers.

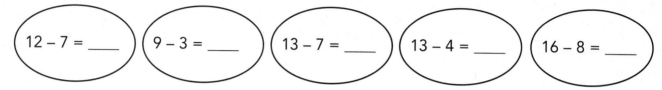

12 – 7 = ____   9 – 3 = ____   13 – 7 = ____   13 – 4 = ____   16 – 8 = ____

5 – 2 = ____   12 – 3 = ____   14 – 8 = ____   12 – 8 = ____   15 – 8 = ____

11 – 8 = ____   13 – 6 = ____   10 – 7 = ____   8 – 3 = ____   9 – 2 = ____

What happens when you subtract an even number from an odd number?

_____

What happens when you subtract an odd number from an even number?

_____

Directions: Even things out! Find and solve only the examples with even answers.

1. 11 – 2 = ____   **6.** 11 – 4 = ____   **11.** 10 – 9 = ____   **16.** 11 – 4 = ____

2. 18 – 9 = ____   **7.** 3 – 0 = ____   **12.** 12 – 5 = ____   **17.** 10 – 3 = ____

3. 7 – 5 = ____   **8.** 14 – 6 = ____   **13.** 0 – 0 = ____   **18.** 11 – 3 = ____

4. 4 – 1 = ____   **9.** 16 – 9 = ____   **14.** 13 – 5 = ____   **19.** 4 – 4 = ____

5. 15 – 7 = ____   **10.** 8 – 3 = ____   **15.** 16 – 7 = ____   **20.** 12 – 7 = ____

What happens when an even number is subtracted from an even number?

_____

What happens when an odd number is subtracted from an odd number?

_____

Mastering Math Facts: Addition and Subtraction © 2009 Richard S. Piccirilli, Scholastic Teaching Resources

Chapter 9

DRILL

STEP 4   Use Meaningful Drill for Subtraction Facts

As with addition facts, students must recall answers to subtraction facts in a reasonable amount of time. Mastering the 100 subtraction facts prepares children for everyday experiences in the real world—from handling simple computations at the cash register to using mental math to calculate how much time is left before a favorite TV show begins.

• A reminder about meaningful drill!

Keep in mind that meaningful drill can take place only when students are ready. The task of committing all 100 subtraction facts to memory is predicated on a student's understanding of the meaning of subtraction and consistent use of the strategies, as well as having had ample time to practice and experience success. Remember, a student's willingness and positive attitude are needed to accomplish mastery. As opposed to premature drill, meaningful drill takes place when students are in a position to be successful as they work to master number facts.

• What are the keys to effective drill sessions?

Drill sessions for subtraction, as for addition, need to be frequent, purposeful, short, and interesting. You should also find ways to reflect upon the sessions. Talk about the results of each drill and acknowledge the steady improvement that students show. It is important, too, to use the results of the drills to guide your work with students on specific facts and patterns they are struggling with.

When students study their missed facts, equip them with specific materials and ideas that will ensure their success. Flash cards, games, and other activities should be a part of a student's remedial process. (Find these and other suggestions for reteaching in Chapters 5 and 10.) Encourage children to share with their classmates how they study missed number facts, and guide them to work collaboratively to master their own subtraction facts. For example, a student can generate a list of troublesome facts, study them, and then ask a partner to quiz him or her. When they take pride in and control of their learning, students are likely to choose the challenging facts that they really need to study.

• What's in this chapter?

You'll find whole-class oral activities to provide more students with added exposure to subtraction combinations. The reproducibles in this chapter underscore the value of additive thinking and help students to build associations among the three numbers that constitute each fact as an aid to mastery.

The one-minute challenges, like those in the addition section, introduce a timed environment in a positive manner. The focus, remember, is on student improvement from one challenge to the next, encouraging each learner to identify which facts he or she needs to study.

Different Kinds of Subtraction Drills

Show students different kinds of drills that are not simply done with pencil and paper—find game-like formats your class enjoys and use them repeatedly.

ACTIVITY 1   Revisit Other Drills

Choose from game ideas, teacher-directed activities, reproducibles, and small-group drills, as well as the online drill sites listed on the Resources page (page 146). Begin by adapting some of the addition-drill activities from Chapter 4 to work on subtraction-fact mastery. These include Combination Roll-Off (page 65), Matchmaker, Matchmaker (page 66), Let's Make an Arrangement (page 67), Slap the Card (page 67), Bingo (page 71), Winner Takes All (page 74), Egg-citing Facts (page 74), and Captured (page 75).

ACTIVITY 2   What Number Is . . .

Copy the combinations below onto the board or an overhead transparency. Call on students to give answers.

Say: *What number is . . .*

2 less than 5 ?	3 less than 6?	9 less than 12?
less than 8?	less than 4?	less than 18?
less than 9?	less than 9?	less than 13?
less than 11?	less than 12?	less than 15?

Variation: With the combinations displayed, ask students for the answers and to announce which strategy was used.

ACTIVITY 3   Double and Triple Subtractions

Use numbers from which you can make two or three subtraction facts. For example: Start with 8, subtract 2 and get 6, from which you then can subtract 4 and at last, subtract 2. Have students tell you what is left by raising a playing card or a Student Response Card. Below are some examples to consider.

MATERIALS
Student Response Cards (page 160) or playing cards (use only cards numbered 1–9 and the Joker for 0)

Say: *10 – 5 – 3* (Answer: 2); *16 – 8 – 2 – 3* (Answer: 3);
12 – 4 – 8 (Answer: 0); *9 – 1 – 5* (Answer: 3);
13 – 5 – 2 – 3 (Answer: 3); *5 – 0 – 5* (Answer: 0);
10 – 3 – 2 (Answer: 5); *17 – 9 – 7* (Answer: 1)

Variation: Have students make up their own examples for the class to solve.

Fast and Focused Subtraction Drill

With Follow Me and We're Going in Circles, you can help students work quickly on subtraction combinations, as you did with addition combinations. You can also use a visual aid to drill subtraction facts.

ACTIVITY 1   Follow Me

Write a minus sign and the chart of numbers listed below onto chart paper, the board, or a transparency. Show it to the class.

1. Say: *Follow me.*
2. Point to the 1 and then the 4.
3. Point to the minus sign
4. Point to the 8.
5. Say: *Now we have 14 – 8.*
6. Ask: *What is the answer?* (6)
7. Continue in this manner with other subtraction combinations, using the numbers listed on the chart, pointing to the minus sign between each.

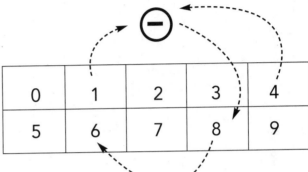

0	1	2	3	4
5	6	7	8	9

Variation: Have students take turns leading the Follow Me exercise.

ACTIVITY 2   We're Going in Circles

Copy circles onto the board or an overhead transparency. Write the minuend in the center and subtrahends on the outside of the circle. As you point to a number outside the circle, ask a volunteer to give the correct answer by subtracting the outside number from the inside number. Use the examples below.

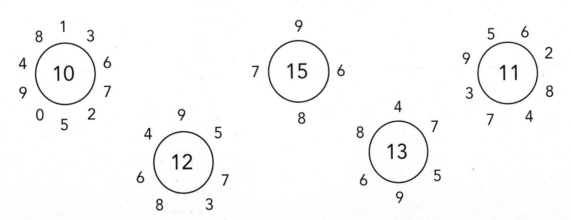

Name _____ Date _____

Match Me!

Directions: Draw lines to match each number combination with its answer.

Hint: Not all the numbers will be used.

Example

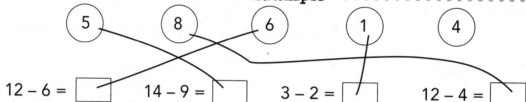

⑤　　⑧　　⑥　　①　　④

12 – 6 = ▭　　14 – 9 = ▭　　3 – 2 = ▭　　12 – 4 = ▭

1.　　⑥　　⑧　　⑨　　③　　⓪

7 – 4 = ▭　　9 – 9 = ▭　　14 – 5 = ▭　　17 – 9 = ▭

2.　　⑧　　④　　⑤　　③　　⑦

12 – 4 = ▭　　14 – 9 = ▭　　13 – 6 = ▭　　9 – 6 = ▭

3.　　②　　④　　⑤　　⑥　　③

6 – 2 = ▭　　5 – 3 = ▭　　6 – 0 = ▭　　8 – 5 = ▭

4.　　④　　⑥　　⑨　　⑤　　⑧

8 – 3 = ▭　　13 – 7 = ▭　　12 – 3 = ▭　　15 – 7 = ▭

Mastering Math Facts: Addition and Subtraction © 2009 Richard S. Piccirilli, Scholastic Teaching Resources

Cards for Subtraction Drill

For fun and hands-on experiences, use playing cards and flash cards to drill students.

. . . .

ACTIVITY 1   Read My Mind

Explain and model the game: Two students face each other. At the same time, each picks a card from the deck, and, without looking at the card, puts it faceup on his or her forehead. Tell the students the sum of the two cards. Each student looks at the other student's card to determine the number on his or her own card. (Explain that students should subtract the other student's card from the total given.) The first student to correctly identify the card wins a point. Play continues until one student wins with a total of 10 points.

MATERIALS
Deck of playing cards with tens and face cards removed

Variation: Students can play in small groups with a third student acting as the teacher.

. . . .

ACTIVITY 2   What's the Hidden Number?

With the construction paper, make a sleeve in which the number fact card can fit. Cover one of the factors and then reveal the answer once a response is given.

MATERIALS
Subtraction and addition flash cards with the facts written horizontally, piece of black or colored construction paper

| 6 + ▌ = 14 | | 12 – 8 = ▌ | | 17 – ▌ = 9 |

. . . .

ACTIVITY 3   One-Minute Challenges

Hand out this series of drill exercises one at a time—over the course of one or two weeks. Each time remind students to do their best and leave blanks for answers they don't know automatically. Have them stop at the end of one minute and circle and write their scores (the number they answered correctly) at the bottom of the page. Ask them to circle any incomplete facts on the page and study these facts to prepare for the next challenge. Have students keep their One-Minute challenges in a folder so that you and they can compare their progress from one Challenge to the next.

MATERIALS
Copy of One-Minute Challenge drills (pages 133–137) for each student

Name _____ Date _____

Find Left-out Louie

Directions: Left-out Louie is the only number in the grid not used to answer any of the subtraction combinations below. Can you find him? Cross out numbers in the grid when you use them as answers.

3	6	2	7	1
7	8	2	4	6
3	8	8	1	5
1	0	9	2	9
0	4	5	9	4

Example

1. 9 – 1 = __8__

2. 12 – 6 = _____

3. 5 – 4 = _____

4. 8 – 8 = _____

5. 12 – 7 = _____

6. 14 – 6 = _____

7. 8 – 5 = _____

8. 18 – 9 = _____

9. 12 – 3 = _____

10. 10 – 4 = _____

11. 14 – 9 = _____

12. 17 – 8 = _____

13. 12 – 5 = _____

14. 4 – 3 = _____

15. 10 – 3 = _____

16. 13 – 9 = _____

17. 2 – 1 = _____

18. 10 – 7 = _____

19. 13 – 5 = _____

20. 11 – 7 = _____

21. 10 – 8 = _____

22. 9 – 5 = _____

23. 11 – 9 = _____

24. 9 – 9 = _____

When you find Left-out Louie, write his number here. _____

Mastering Math Facts: Addition and Subtraction © 2009 Richard S. Piccirilli, Scholastic Teaching Resources

Name _____ Date _____

Subtraction One-Minute Challenge #1

Directions: In one minute, complete as many combinations as you can. At first, you may not be able to do them all. Do your best and try to improve your score for the next challenge.

Hint: If you don't know an answer, leave it blank. When you finish, look for the combinations you left blank so you can study them for the next time.

	a	b	c	d	e	f
1.	4 − 3	9 − 9	7 − 6	6 − 1	7 − 5	9 − 0
2.	8 − 2	12 − 7	8 − 1	14 − 5	15 − 9	6 − 6
3.	12 − 4	1 − 1	14 − 7	10 − 1	12 − 6	8 − 5
4.	6 − 3	17 − 8	11 − 4	17 − 9	12 − 8	11 − 6
5.	4 − 4	13 − 5	0 − 0	8 − 3	13 − 8	16 − 9

$$\frac{}{30} \quad \frac{\text{Number correct}}{\text{Total}}$$

Mastering Math Facts: Addition and Subtraction © 2009 Richard S. Piccirilli, Scholastic Teaching Resources

Name _____ Date _____

Subtraction One-Minute Challenge #2

Directions: In one minute, complete as many combinations as you can. At first, you may not be able to do them all. Do your best and try to improve your score for the next challenge.

Hint: If you don't know an answer, leave it blank. When you finish, look for the combinations you left blank so you can study them for the next time.

	a	b	c	d	e	f
1.	6 − 2	14 − 7	9 − 5	5 − 2	15 − 8	9 − 0
2.	16 − 8	10 − 8	7 − 7	0 − 0	11 − 5	15 − 6
3.	3 − 2	14 − 9	13 − 8	13 − 6	8 − 2	14 − 8
4.	12 − 3	11 − 9	11 − 6	13 − 7	17 − 8	13 − 4
5.	11 − 4	3 − 3	10 − 3	3 − 0	1 − 1	14 − 5

$\dfrac{}{30}$ **Number correct**
Total

Mastering Math Facts: Addition and Subtraction © 2009 Richard S. Piccirilli, Scholastic Teaching Resources

Name _____ Date _____

Subtraction One-Minute Challenge #3

Directions: In one minute, complete as many combinations as you can. At the end, compare how you did with Challenges 1 and 2.

Hint: If you don't know an answer, leave it blank. When you finish, look for the combinations you left blank so you can study them for the next time.

	a	b	c	d	e	f
1.	2 − 0	6 − 2	13 − 6	16 − 7	14 − 9	1 − 0
2.	8 − 3	10 − 5	3 − 1	15 − 9	14 − 8	13 − 8
3.	11 − 7	10 − 6	4 − 0	12 − 4	11 − 5	16 − 8
4.	13 − 5	7 − 6	11 − 3	12 − 9	8 − 5	13 − 4
5.	17 − 8	14 − 7	9 − 8	14 − 5	16 − 9	13 − 7

$$\frac{\text{Number correct}}{\text{Total}} \quad \overline{30}$$

Name _____ Date _____

Subtraction One-Minute Challenge #4

Directions: In one minute, complete as many combinations as you can. At the end, compare how you did with Challenges 1, 2, and 3.

Hint: If you don't know an answer, leave it blank. When you finish, look for the combinations you left blank so you can study them for the next Challenge.

	a	b	c	d	e	f
1.	10 – 5	8 – 6	3 – 0	12 – 5	2 – 2	13 – 6
2.	15 – 8	11 – 9	14 – 8	6 – 4	15 – 7	14 – 6
3.	11 – 5	4 – 0	6 – 6	17 – 9	9 – 3	12 – 4
4.	8 – 5	13 – 9	11 – 3	10 – 7	17 – 8	10 – 8
5.	18 – 9	7 – 4	9 – 6	13 – 7	16 – 9	11 – 4

$$\frac{}{30} \quad \frac{\textbf{Number correct}}{\textbf{Total}}$$

Mastering Math Facts: Addition and Subtraction © 2009 Richard S. Piccirilli, Scholastic Teaching Resources

Name _____ Date _____

Subtraction One-Minute Challenge #5

Directions: In one minute, complete as many combinations as you can. At the end, compare how you did with Challenges 1, 2, 3, and 4.

Hint: If you don't know an answer, leave it blank. When you finish, look for the combinations you left blank so you can study them.

	a	b	c	d	e	f
1.	9 − 5	6 − 6	13 − 9	5 − 0	9 − 2	8 − 3
2.	12 − 8	10 − 8	11 − 8	11 − 2	16 − 9	14 − 8
3.	11 − 7	7 − 2	8 − 2	12 − 4	9 − 3	14 − 7
4.	12 − 5	9 − 8	13 − 7	10 − 4	11 − 9	11 − 3
5.	11 − 6	10 − 6	12 − 7	7 − 3	14 − 9	15 − 9

$$\frac{}{30} \quad \frac{\text{Number correct}}{\text{Total}}$$

Chapter 10

ASSESSMENT AND RETEACHING

STEP 5 Practical Diagnosis and Remediation of Subtraction Facts

If you have not yet read the Addition section, please look back to Chapter 5 (see pages 82–86) to find details on how to provide practical diagnosis and remediation of subtraction facts. In that chapter, you will find background on meaningful assessment of number-fact mastery and tools that help you determine when and how to administer Practice Tests and Diagnostic Tests. You'll also find progress sheets and reteaching tips.

What is most important to remember when you are administering either a practice test or diagnostic test, is that you must lead the activity rather than have students do the assessments independently. Taking the time to properly administer the tests will positively impact your students' long-term mastery of number facts.

• What's in this chapter?

The chapter contains five practice tests, one diagnostic test, and a diagnostic summary sheet. Specific diagnostic and remedial techniques and tools for recording progress are found in Chapter 5.

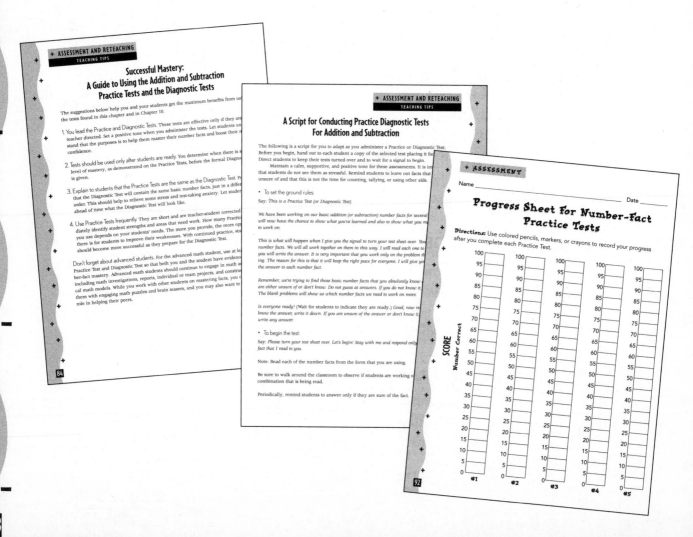

Name _____ Date _____

Subtraction Practice Test #1

	a	b	c	d	e	f	g	h	i	j
1.	6 – 1	13 – 7	7 – 5	7 – 0	13 – 4	11 – 8	6 – 2	9 – 9	14 – 6	4 – 3
2.	9 – 8	12 – 7	7 – 4	3 – 1	11 – 3	12 – 5	6 – 6	9 – 0	8 – 2	13 – 9
3.	8 – 1	9 – 7	10 – 6	3 – 3	7 – 2	14 – 5	15 – 9	5 – 4	3 – 0	16 – 8
4.	4 – 2	12 – 4	1 – 1	7 – 3	14 – 7	8 – 8	10 – 1	12 – 6	14 – 9	8 – 5
5.	6 – 3	2 – 0	7 – 6	10 – 5	2 – 2	17 – 8	11 – 7	11 – 4	7 – 1	17 – 9
6.	4 – 1	12 – 8	9 – 3	6 – 5	9 – 2	11 – 6	16 – 7	4 – 4	11 – 9	8 – 0
7.	11 – 2	13 – 5	10 – 7	2 – 1	0 – 0	16 – 9	8 – 6	8 – 3	14 – 8	8 – 4
8.	9 – 6	7 – 7	6 – 4	10 – 9	5 – 1	15 – 8	12 – 3	5 – 3	11 – 5	10 – 2
9.	1 – 0	15 – 7	10 – 3	9 – 5	10 – 8	9 – 4	6 – 0	12 – 9	15 – 6	3 – 2
10.	9 – 1	4 – 0	13 – 6	8 – 7	5 – 0	5 – 5	13 – 8	5 – 2	18 – 9	10 – 4

Number correct
_____
100   Total

Name _____ Date _____

Subtraction Practice Test #2

	a	b	c	d	e
1.	7 – 4 = ____	3 – 0 = ____	10 – 1 = ____	8 – 0 = ____	12 – 8 = ____
2.	10 – 3 = ____	14 – 5 = ____	1 – 1 = ____	6 – 1 = ____	12 – 9 = ____
3.	9 – 4 = ____	5 – 4 = ____	8 – 5 = ____	10 – 7 = ____	6 – 6 = ____
4.	11 – 3 = ____	3 – 3 = ____	9 – 6 = ____	9 – 1 = ____	13 – 5 = ____
5.	2 – 0 = ____	8 – 7 = ____	4 – 4 = ____	11 – 4 = ____	8 – 4 = ____
6.	13 – 7 = ____	10 – 4 = ____	13 – 4 = ____	9 – 8 = ____	5 – 1 = ____
7.	11 – 7 = ____	5 – 3 = ____	13 – 9 = ____	15 – 7 = ____	7 – 3 = ____
8.	8 – 1 = ____	10 – 2 = ____	17 – 9 = ____	11 – 8 = ____	11 – 6 = ____
9.	4 – 3 = ____	8 – 2 = ____	11 – 9 = ____	4 – 2 = ____	8 – 8 = ____
10.	6 – 3 = ____	12 – 7 = ____	6 – 4 = ____	16 – 7 = ____	8 – 6 = ____
11.	7 – 1 = ____	16 – 9 = ____	18 – 9 = ____	2 – 1 = ____	10 – 6 = ____
12.	4 – 1 = ____	14 – 9 = ____	6 – 0 = ____	13 – 6 = ____	14 – 6 = ____
13.	17 – 8 = ____	12 – 3 = ____	7 – 5 = ____	9 – 7 = ____	5 – 5 = ____
14.	13 – 8 = ____	1 – 0 = ____	14 – 8 = ____	7 – 6 = ____	2 – 2 = ____
15.	11 – 5 = ____	8 – 3 = ____	3 – 2 = ____	10 – 9 = ____	15 – 6 = ____
16.	4 – 0 = ____	7 – 7 = ____	9 – 2 = ____	7 – 0 = ____	5 – 0 = ____
17.	16 – 8 = ____	0 – 0 = ____	12 – 6 = ____	10 – 8 = ____	7 – 2 = ____
18.	9 – 0 = ____	15 – 9 = ____	10 – 5 = ____	12 – 5 = ____	5 – 2 = ____
19.	15 – 8 = ____	9 – 5 = ____	11 – 2 = ____	9 – 3 = ____	12 – 4 = ____
20.	14 – 7 = ____	6 – 5 = ____	9 – 9 = ____	3 – 1 = ____	6 – 2 = ____

Number correct

$\dfrac{}{100}$ Total

Name _____   Date _____

Subtraction Practice Test #3

	a	b	c	d	e	f	g	h	i	j
1.	6 − 2	2 − 0	12 − 3	6 − 0	13 − 6	8 − 6	16 − 7	14 − 9	9 − 7	9 − 0
2.	8 − 3	9 − 2	12 − 6	7 − 2	12 − 5	5 − 0	9 − 5	15 − 8	10 − 5	9 − 4
3.	3 − 1	7 − 3	15 − 9	11 − 9	14 − 8	13 − 8	1 − 1	6 − 4	7 − 1	14 − 6
4.	4 − 3	11 − 7	5 − 3	15 − 7	10 − 4	8 − 4	11 − 6	8 − 0	10 − 6	12 − 7
5.	16 − 8	8 − 2	12 − 4	9 − 3	0 − 0	4 − 0	3 − 2	11 − 5	17 − 9	11 − 8
6.	1 − 0	3 − 3	13 − 9	12 − 8	13 − 5	9 − 1	12 − 9	5 − 1	2 − 2	13 − 4
7.	7 − 0	7 − 6	7 − 7	15 − 6	5 − 5	2 − 1	4 − 4	8 − 5	5 − 4	6 − 6
8.	11 − 3	3 − 0	10 − 1	8 − 8	10 − 7	8 − 7	10 − 3	6 − 3	10 − 2	7 − 5
9.	6 − 1	17 − 8	10 − 9	5 − 2	10 − 8	11 − 2	6 − 5	14 − 7	9 − 8	14 − 5
10.	8 − 1	7 − 4	4 − 2	4 − 1	16 − 9	18 − 9	9 − 9	9 − 6	11 − 4	13 − 7

Mastering Math Facts: Addition and Subtraction © 2009 Richard S. Piccirilli, Scholastic Teaching Resources

Number correct
___
100   Total

Name _____ Date _____

Subtraction Practice Test #4

	a	b	c	d	e	f	g	h	i	j
1.	4 − 1	16 − 9	8 − 1	9 − 6	11 − 7	9 − 4	7 − 4	13 − 7	18 − 9	4 − 2
2.	10 − 9	5 − 2	17 − 8	6 − 1	11 − 2	6 − 5	14 − 5	9 − 8	14 − 7	10 − 8
3.	3 − 0	8 − 7	11 − 3	10 − 3	6 − 3	7 − 5	10 − 2	8 − 8	10 − 7	10 − 1
4.	7 − 6	4 − 4	5 − 4	7 − 0	5 − 5	8 − 5	2 − 1	15 − 6	13 − 9	7 − 7
5.	6 − 6	1 − 1	12 − 8	9 − 1	5 − 1	3 − 3	2 − 0	13 − 4	12 − 9	13 − 5
6.	11 − 5	17 − 9	11 − 8	4 − 0	16 − 8	9 − 3	8 − 2	12 − 4	0 − 0	3 − 2
7.	4 − 3	15 − 7	5 − 3	11 − 4	11 − 6	10 − 6	12 − 7	8 − 0	8 − 4	10 − 4
8.	3 − 1	15 − 9	7 − 3	11 − 9	14 − 8	13 − 8	1 − 0	6 − 4	7 − 1	14 − 6
9.	9 − 9	2 − 2	9 − 5	12 − 3	9 − 2	13 − 6	7 − 2	8 − 3	5 − 0	15 − 8
10.	6 − 2	10 − 5	6 − 0	8 − 6	16 − 7	14 − 9	9 − 7	9 − 0	12 − 5	12 − 6

Mastering Math Facts: Addition and Subtraction © 2009 Richard S. Piccirilli, Scholastic Teaching Resources

Number correct
100   **Total**

Name _____ Date _____

Subtraction Practice Test #5

	a	b	c	d	e	f	g	h	i	j
1.	8 − 7	12 − 3	10 − 7	9 − 9	14 − 5	11 − 7	12 − 4	2 − 2	14 − 6	1 − 1
2.	8 − 6	7 − 2	16 − 9	15 − 6	12 − 6	8 − 0	7 − 4	13 − 9	18 − 9	17 − 8
3.	1 − 0	9 − 7	13 − 6	10 − 9	9 − 0	6 − 6	9 − 1	6 − 3	10 − 3	17 − 9
4.	10 − 5	10 − 8	8 − 4	13 − 7	5 − 1	8 − 8	8 − 1	8 − 3	9 − 4	15 − 7
5.	4 − 3	7 − 1	6 − 4	10 − 6	14 − 8	9 − 6	13 − 4	6 − 0	12 − 5	10 − 2
6.	13 − 5	4 − 0	3 − 0	5 − 2	11 − 8	0 − 0	12 − 9	12 − 8	15 − 8	5 − 0
7.	6 − 1	16 − 8	3 − 2	9 − 2	3 − 1	7 − 5	5 − 5	13 − 8	9 − 8	7 − 0
8.	10 − 4	15 − 9	5 − 3	3 − 3	12 − 7	9 − 5	14 − 7	11 − 2	7 − 3	6 − 2
9.	4 − 1	16 − 7	2 − 1	10 − 1	7 − 7	11 − 4	2 − 0	6 − 5	7 − 6	11 − 3
10.	5 − 4	8 − 5	8 − 2	4 − 2	11 − 5	9 − 3	11 − 9	11 − 6	4 − 4	14 − 9

Number correct

$\dfrac{}{100}$ Total

Name _____ Date _____

Subtraction Diagnostic Test

	a	b	c	d	e	f	g	h	i	j
1.	6 – 2	2 – 2	12 – 3	6 – 0	13 – 6	8 – 6	16 – 7	14 – 9	9 – 7	9 – 0
2.	7 – 3	5 – 4	12 – 7	3 – 0	15 – 9	14 – 5	10 – 6	8 – 1	8 – 8	11 – 3
3.	11 – 6	8 – 0	3 – 1	7 – 4	8 – 4	9 – 8	16 – 8	9 – 9	13 – 7	10 – 4
4.	11 – 9	1 – 0	12 – 5	8 – 5	15 – 7	10 – 1	14 – 7	10 – 5	4 – 2	5 – 3
5.	11 – 7	3 – 2	4 – 4	7 – 2	6 – 5	8 – 2	4 – 1	12 – 4	2 – 1	9 – 3
6.	10 – 7	0 – 0	5 – 5	4 – 0	18 – 9	12 – 6	11 – 2	5 – 2	15 – 6	16 – 9
7.	10 – 3	15 – 8	10 – 8	11 – 5	9 – 4	17 – 9	8 – 7	14 – 8	7 – 7	11 – 8
8.	4 – 3	9 – 1	10 – 2	9 – 2	12 – 9	1 – 1	9 – 6	8 – 3	10 – 9	12 – 8
9.	3 – 3	5 – 1	5 – 0	7 – 6	13 – 9	6 – 3	13 – 5	17 – 8	13 – 8	11 – 4
10.	7 – 1	2 – 0	6 – 4	13 – 4	7 – 0	7 – 5	6 – 6	14 – 6	6 – 1	9 – 5

Number correct

100 / Total

Mastering Math Facts: Addition and Subtraction © 2009 Richard S. Piccirilli, Scholastic Teaching Resources

Name _____ Date _____

Subtraction Diagnostic Summary Sheet

Directions: Use your Diagnostic Test to show what you know! Draw a 🙂 or ☆ for all the number facts that you answered correctly. For each fact you didn't answer correctly, leave it blank. These are the facts you'll need to study!

Subtraction Facts I Know!

–	0	1	2	3	4	5	6	7	8	9	10	11	12	13	14	15	16	17	18
0																			
1																			
2																			
3																			
4																			
5																			
6																			
7																			
8																			
9																			

Number correct _____

Appendix

Resources for Teaching Addition and Subtraction Facts

- ### Children's Literature

Stories, illustrations, and discussions stimulate students' thinking and help them focus on math. Picture books can help students better understand the addition and subtraction processes. These are some examples:

Cleary, B. (2004). *The mission of addition.* New York: Millbrook Press.
Children learn the process of addition through pictures and interesting rhymes.

Giganti, P. (1989). *How many snails?* New York: Greenwillow Books.
Questions with pictures for counting leads to concepts related to addition and subtraction.

Leedy, L. (1997). *Mission: addition.* New York: Holiday House.
Illustrated scenes show visual story problems. Addition is used in various situations.

Leedy, L. (2000). *Subtraction action.* New York: Holiday House.
Definitions of remainders and differences, as well as writing subtraction sentences, are part of this illustrated book with animal characters.

Long, L. (1996). *Domino addition.* Watertown, PA: Charlesbridge.
This very simple and basic concept book moves from counting to addition.

- ### Online Resources

There are numerous Web sites that emphasize drill. Once students are ready, online drill can be motivating to children. The following are Web sites to explore.

AAA Math. Retrieved on January 15, 2009 from http://www.aaamath.com
Find drill activities with a time component. Students can set their own time limit as a challenge. You may need to first guide students on this site.

A Plus Math. Retrieved on January 15, 2009 from http://www.aplusmath.com
There are flash-card drills, including personalized, printable flash cards.

CoolMath.com. Retrieved on January 15, 2009 from http://www.coolmath.com
This kid-friendly site has math lessons on making meaning as well as practice and drill activities.

Math.com. Retrieved on January 15, 2009 from http://www.math.com
Find drill activities that go beyond the number facts, plus timed drills.

Songs for Teaching. Retrieved on January 15, 2009 from http://www.songsforteaching.com
This site offers a variety of songs to teach number-fact learning.

ANSWER KEY

Page 19: *Story Problems You Can Solve*

1. 12

2. 16

3. 10

4. Kay

5. Yes

6. Jets

Page 20: *Writing Story Problems for Addition Facts*
Answers will vary.

Page 24: *Zero the Hero*
Row 1: 2, 7, 6, 3, 5, 7
Row 2: 9, 4, 1, 8, 2, 5
Row 3: 4, 6, 9, 1, 8, 0
Possible answer: Zero is a hero because it makes adding easy. When zero is an addend, the answer is the same as the other addend.

Page 28: *10 Is a Friend*
Row 1: $8 + 3 = 10 + 1$, $4 + 7 = 1 + 10$
Row 2: $7 + 5 = 10 + 2$, $5 + 8 = 10 + 3$, $3 + 8 = 1 + 10$
Row 3: $8 + 5 = 10 + 3$, $8 + 4 = 10 + 2$, $7 + 5 = 10 + 2$
Row 3: $6 + 8 = 4 + 10$, $4 + 8 = 2 + 10$

Page 33: *Detective Work*

Zero the Hero	Adding One More
0 + 5	5 + 1
0 + 3	1 + 6
0 + 4	2 + 1
0 + 0	8 + 1
2 + 0	1 + 4
0 + 8	6 + 1

Almost-Doubles	Speedy 9s
7 + 8	4 + 9
6 + 7	9 + 5
7 + 6	9 + 7
8 + 7	7 + 9
3 + 4	3 + 9
5 + 6	9 + 6

10 Again
8 + 5
5 + 7
8 + 3
4 + 8
8 + 6
6 + 8

Page 41: *Number, Please*

1. 14

2. 16

3. 11

4. 5

5. 5

6. 13

7. 18

8. 17

Page 42: *Writing Story Problems*
Answers will vary.

Page 43: *Sum Circle Puzzle*
For the sums of 8, 9 and 10, the center numbers are 1, 3 and 5 respectively. Accept correct answers, but make sure that the center number is correct.

Page 44: *Number Search*

1. 1, 9; 6, 4

2. 6, 7; 4, 9

3. 1, 0

4. 5, 4; 9, 0

5. 5, 9

6. 6, 9

7. 7, 9

8. 1, 5, 9;
   5, 6, 4
   6, 9, 0

Page 45: *What's Missing? Part 1*
Sum 1: 0
Sum 2: 0, 1, 2
Sum 3: 3, 2, 2, 3
Sum 4: 0, 1, 2, 1, 0
Sum 5: 0, 4, 2, 3, 1, 5
Sum 6: 0, 1, 4, 3, 2, 5, 0
Sum 7: 7, 6, 5, 3, 4, 2, 1, 0
Sum 8: 8, 1, 6, 3, 4, 5, 2, 7, 8
Sum 9: 0, 8, 2, 5, 4, 4, 6, 7, 1
Sum 10: 1, 8, 3, 4, 5, 4, 3, 8, 9
Possible answer: I noticed that the numbers went up to get to each sum.

Page 46: *What's Missing? Part 2*
Sum 11: 2, 8, 4, 5, 5, 4, 8, 9
Sum 12: 9, 8, 5, 6, 7, 4, 3
Sum 13: 4, 5, 7, 6, 5, 9
Sum 14: 9, 8, 7, 8, 9
Sum 15: 6, 8, 7, 9
Sum 16: 9, 8, 9
Sum 17: 8, 9
Sum 18: 9
Possible answer: I found that the top and bottom equations in each box had the same numbers.

Page 47: *Point It Out!*

1. ◀

2. ▶

3. ◀

4. ▶

5. ◀

6. =

7. =

8. ▶

9. =

10. ▶

11. ▶

12. =

Page 48: *A, B, C: Which Is the Largest of the Three?*

1. C	**5.** B	**9.** C
2. B	**6.** A	**10.** C
3. C	**7.** C	**11.** A
4. A	**8.** B	**12.** A

Page 49: *Find the Triplets*

2, 4, 5, 7, 8, 10, 12, 13, 14, 15

Page 50: *Valuable Words*

1. 11	**7.** 13
2. 15	**8.** 9
3. 11	**9.** 11
4. 13	**10.** 16
5. 11	**11.** 15
6. 8	**12.** 7

The most valuable word: Deb

The least valuable word: Ed

Page 51: *Breaking Up Is Easy*

Answers may vary. Possible combinations include:

1. 3 + 3 + 7 = 13 **or** 6 + 4 + 3 = 13;
   3 + 3 + 4 + 3 = 13 **or** 4 + 2 + 5 + 2 = 13

2. 6 + 3 + 7 = 16 **or** 5 + 4 + 7 = 16;
   6 + 3 + 4 + 3 = 16 **or** 5 + 4 + 5 + 2 = 16

3. 4 + 4 + 5 = 13 **or** 6 + 2 + 5 = 13;
   4 + 4 + 3 + 2 = 13 **or** 2 + 6 + 3 + 2 = 13

4. 3 + 4 + 4 = 1 **or** 7 + 2 + 2 = 11;
   3 + 4 + 2 + 2 = 11 **or** 5 + 2 + 3 + 1 = 11

Challenge: Answers will vary but may include:

12 = 3 + 4 + 5

14 = 3 + 6 + 5

15 = 2 + 5 + 8

Page 52: *Number Facts in Disguise, Part 1:*

1. 10	**7.** 16
2. 14	**8.** 15
3. 13	**9.** 11
4. 12	**10.** 11
5. 14	**11.** 9
6. 16	**12.** 12

Page 53: *Number Facts in Disguise, Part 2*

1. 7, 12	**6.** 7, 5, 12
2. 7, 13	**7.** 6, 8, 14
3. 8, 12	**8.** 6, 14
4. 7, 13	**9.** 8, 12
5. 7, 15	**10.** 7, 14

Page 55: *Follow the Rules*

Add 5	Add 9	Add 1
8	12	9
14	16	3
12	15	8
10	17	7
13	13	5

Add 7	Add 2	Add 4
16	9	10
13	8	11
15	6	9
12	10	13
11	11	12

Add 6	Add 3	Add 8
12	9	11
10	11	15
15	8	12
13	12	13
14	10	16

Page 56: *Numbers Are Shaping Up*

(Answers include reversals of addends listed below, as well.)

1–4. 2 + 9, 3 + 8, 4 + 7, 5 + 6

5. 6 + 6

6–8. 3 + 9, 4 + 8, 5 + 7, 6 + 6

9–11. 4 + 9, 5 + 8, 6 + 7

12. 7 + 7

Page 57: *Fill the Holes*

Addend	*4*	7	6	7	8	*8*	7	7
Addend	2	3	*6*	5	*8*	4	6	*4*
Sum	6	*10*	12	*12*	16	12	*13*	11

Addend	9	5	*9*	*9*	9	5	7	4
Addend	6	*8*	4	8	*9*	6	*9*	5
Sum	*15*	13	13	17	18	*11*	16	*9*

Addend	*6*	8	7	7	3	7	*6*	3
Addend	4	4	*3*	*8*	9	*7*	3	*5*
Sum	10	12	10	15	12	14	9	8

Addend	*8*	7	9	4	0	2	*5*	*6*
Addend	6	2	*5*	7	*9*	7	3	0
Sum	14	9	14	*11*	9	*9*	8	6

Page 58: *The Function Machine*

A. 6, 8, 8

B. 7, 3, 6

C. 6, 15, 8

D. 5, 7, 4

Page 65: *Combination Roll-Off*

Answers will vary.

Page 72: *We're Going in Circles*

7 Circle	**3 Circle**
7 + 6 = 13	3 + 0 = 3
7 + 1 = 8	3 + 4 = 7
7 + 0 = 7	3 + 9 = 12
7 + 8 = 15	3 + 6 = 9
7 + 7 = 14	3 + 5 = 8
7 + 5 = 12	3 + 8 = 11

8 Circle

8 + 4 = 12
8 + 8 = 16
8 + 6 = 14
8 + 5 = 13
8 + 7 = 15
8 + 9 = 17

0 Circle

0 + 5 = 5
0 + 0 = 0
0 + 1 = 1
0 + 8 = 8
0 + 7 = 7
0 + 6 = 6

6 Circle

6 + 2 = 8
6 + 4 = 10
6 + 7 = 13
6 + 3 = 9
6 + 6 = 12
6 + 8 = 14

2 Circle

2 + 3 = 5
2 + 8 = 10
2 + 9 = 11
2 + 7 = 9
2 + 5 = 7
2 + 6 = 8

9 Circle

9 + 1 = 10
9 + 8 = 17
9 + 6 = 15
9 + 5 = 14
9 + 7 = 16
9 + 4 = 13

4 Circle

4 + 0 = 4
4 + 8 = 12
4 + 7 = 11
4 + 9 = 13
4 + 5 = 9
4 + 6 = 10

Page 73: *Hi, Partner!*

1. 7, 8, 7, 2, 6
2. 11, 12, 9, 10, 9
3. 14, 18, 13, 10, 9
4. 8, 9, 10, 8, 13
5. 11, 13, 12, 11, 7

Page 76: *Addition One-Minute Challenge #1*

	a	b	c	d	e	f
1.	8	8	3	0	8	10
2.	17	13	15	13	16	14
3.	18	11	16	12	6	15
4.	10	12	11	14	5	2
5.	12	1	11	13	11	10

Page 77: *Addition One-Minute Challenge #2*

	a	b	c	d	e	f
1.	8	8	9	9	8	9
2.	10	10	12	11	11	1
3.	12	10	7	13	11	12
4.	7	7	15	8	9	9
5.	1	7	6	6	13	7

Page 78: *Addition One-Minute Challenge #3*

	a	b	c	d	e	f
1.	5	11	10	8	8	9
2.	11	12	6	12	10	9
3.	12	5	11	7	10	11
4.	9	2	4	4	9	8
5.	11	11	2	15	8	6

Page 79: *Addition One-Minute Challenge #4*

	a	b	c	d	e	f
1.	10	7	3	10	9	11
2.	8	4	4	12	14	15
3.	1	4	12	4	5	2
4.	10	14	17	14	4	11
5.	7	9	18	15	7	7

Page 80: *Addition One-Minute Challenge #5*

	a	b	c	d	e	f
1.	2	4	4	5	5	7
2.	15	2	11	5	13	8
3.	10	8	11	6	12	10
4.	16	14	16	10	9	6
5.	11	13	7	13	8	8

Page 81: *Show Off!*

+	5	3	7	0	1	8	4	9	2	6
2	7	5	9	2	3	10	6	11	4	8
4	9	7	11	4	5	12	8	13	6	10
0	5	3	7	0	1	8	4	9	2	6
6	11	9	13	6	7	14	10	15	8	12
1	6	4	8	1	2	9	5	10	3	7
9	14	12	16	9	10	17	13	18	11	15
5	10	8	12	5	6	13	9	14	7	11
3	8	6	10	3	4	11	7	12	5	9
7	12	10	14	7	8	15	11	16	9	13
8	13	11	15	8	9	16	12	17	10	14

Page 87: *Addition Practice Test #1*

	a	b	c	d	e	f	g	h	i	j
1.	9	12	3	12	8	13	6	11	9	7
2.	14	8	9	7	15	10	16	3	5	3
3.	10	14	4	14	12	7	8	12	1	8
4.	16	9	11	11	9	12	4	8	6	4
5.	11	16	8	8	14	8	0	13	2	10
6.	18	13	5	13	10	4	9	5	8	5
7.	15	10	10	9	6	9	1	15	3	12
8.	12	15	6	5	11	5	7	10	10	9
9.	17	11	2	10	7	11	17	2	7	6
10.	13	7	7	6	13	6	9	14	4	11

Page 88: *Addition Practice Test #2*

	a	b	c	d	e
1.	10	17	14	6	5
2.	3	14	7	13	9
3.	7	13	9	7	1
4.	16	17	8	5	6
5.	14	8	0	10	13
6.	3	3	7	16	9
7.	11	5	6	6	5
8.	15	8	8	13	8
9.	8	6	12	3	9
10.	10	7	12	11	10
11.	5	15	13	16	10
12.	2	11	12	11	10
13.	12	14	1	12	4
14.	2	4	4	7	9
15.	14	2	8	6	4
16.	9	11	15	4	9
17.	11	18	9	8	13
18.	11	9	10	15	7
19.	6	12	11	7	10
20.	10	5	8	9	12

Page 89: *Addition Practice Test #3*

	a	b	c	d	e	f	g	h	i	j
1.	8	8	9	9	0	8	9	11	8	10
2.	10	10	12	11	11	1	9	10	12	6
3.	12	10	7	13	11	12	10	12	11	5
4.	3	13	13	12	3	14	11	6	14	17
5.	14	16	16	12	15	3	15	18	14	10
6.	10	7	2	7	3	4	8	9	9	17
7.	9	6	5	4	4	8	14	8	13	5
8.	13	5	10	16	6	8	11	11	2	15
9.	1	7	6	6	13	7	6	7	5	5
10.	7	7	15	8	9	9	9	4	4	2

Page 90: *Addition Practice Test #4*

	a	b	c	d	e	f	g	h	i	j
1.	8	11	10	8	8	9	9	0	9	8
2.	11	12	6	12	10	9	1	11	10	10
3.	12	5	11	7	10	11	13	12	10	12
4.	3	17	14	11	6	3	13	13	12	14
5.	3	14	16	16	12	15	15	18	14	10
6.	10	17	9	7	2	7	3	4	8	9
7.	8	14	8	5	13	9	6	5	4	4
8.	11	11	2	15	8	6	16	10	5	13
9.	1	7	6	5	5	7	7	6	13	6
10.	9	2	4	4	9	8	9	7	7	15

Page 91: *Addition Practice Test #5*

	a	b	c	d	e
1.	6	4	5	9	13
2.	9	0	4	14	11
3.	15	11	9	12	7
4.	3	12	11	11	3
5.	5	5	7	8	13
6.	5	8	4	16	3
7.	10	6	13	10	17
8.	6	11	12	18	9
9.	17	6	13	7	9
10.	8	2	12	14	11
11.	9	15	10	7	10
12.	13	9	6	7	10
13.	6	7	8	7	2
14.	4	1	16	4	16
15.	9	6	14	11	2
16.	1	12	12	10	14
17.	10	8	5	14	9
18.	15	12	7	10	13
19.	8	8	8	5	11
20.	15	10	8	3	9

Page 93: *Addition Diagnostic Test*

	a	b	c	d	e	f	g	h	i	j
1.	8	8	3	0	8	10	9	8	7	6
2.	9	7	3	9	6	7	6	2	8	9
3.	8	9	6	10	8	5	9	9	7	7
4.	6	9	7	5	5	7	8	3	13	5
5.	10	7	3	10	9	11	9	6	2	5
6.	8	4	4	12	14	15	4	12	4	1
7.	12	1	11	13	11	10	13	12	11	10
8.	10	12	11	14	5	2	15	11	16	12
9.	18	11	16	12	6	15	14	13	11	4
10.	17	13	15	10	13	16	14	17	14	10

Page 100: *Subtraction Story Problems*

1. 4
2. 6
3. 9
4. 5
5. 7
6. 9
7. 8
8. 5

Page 101: *Writing Story Problems for Subtraction Facts*
Answers will vary.

Page 102: *Fill in the Missing Minuend*

1. 9 10 10 9 8 15
2. 11 12 15 13 11 14
3. 11 8 12 13 3 14
4. 14 8 10 15 4 11
5. 13 12 16 9 10 10
6. 17 16 12 11 8 14

Page 103: *Taller Towers*

1. 2 2. 3 3. 4 4. 4
5. 7 6. 6 7. 7 8. 7

Page 109: *Subtracting With Zero the Hero*

1. 9 2 1 7 6 8 0 3
2. The difference is the same as the minuend.
3. Answers will vary.
4. 0 0 0 0 0 0 0 0
5. The difference is zero.
6. Answers will vary.

Page 110: *Go Back One!*

5, 3, 1, 7, 6, 2, 0, 4, 8

Speedy 9s for Subtraction

1. 2, 3
2. 7, 8
3. 4, 5
4. 6, 7
5. 8, 9
6. 1, 2
7. 3, 4
8. 5, 6
9. The difference is one more than the number in the ones place of the minuend.
10. With addition, the answer is one less. With subtraction, the answer is one more.

Page 112: *Speeding Up Subtraction #1*

1. 1 3 6 4 8 8
2. 3 5 0 6 7 9
3. 4 4 5 2 2 2

Page 113: *Speeding Up Subtraction #2*

1. 3 0 6 7 0 8
2. 0 9 0 0 5 0
3. 5 4 0 3 0 0

Page 116: *Using Subtraction Facts to Solve Problems*

1. 2; 12–10   2. 6; 13–7   3. 8; 17–9
4. 9; 16–7   5. 3; 5–2   6. 7; 12–5

Page 117: *Plug-Ins*

What's in the Pot?

1. 2   2. 6   3. 5   4. 6   5. 3

How Much Change Do You Get?

1. 4   2. 1   3. 2   4. 4   5. 3

How Many Are Girls?

1. 7   2. 4   3. 8   4. 9   5. 9

Page 119: *A Family of Facts*

1. $6 + 8 = 14$
    $8 + 6 = 14$
    $14 - 6 = 8$
    $14 - 8 = 6$

2. $6 + 7 = 13$
    $7 + 6 = 13$
    $13 - 6 = 7$
    $13 - 7 = 6$

3. $7 + 8 = 15$
    $8 + 7 = 15$
    $15 - 7 = 8$
    $15 - 8 = 7$

4. $9 + 8 = 17$
    $8 + 9 = 17$
    $17 - 9 = 8$
    $17 - 8 = 9$

5. $3 + 9 = 12$
    $9 + 3 = 12$
    $12 - 3 = 9$
    $12 - 9 = 3$

6. $7 + 5 = 12$
    $5 + 7 = 12$
    $12 - 7 = 5$
    $12 - 5 = 7$

7. $4 + 9 = 13$
    $9 + 4 = 13$
    $13 - 4 = 9$
    $13 - 9 = 4$

8. $9 + 6 = 15$
    $6 + 9 = 15$
    $15 - 9 = 6$
    $15 - 6 = 9$

Page 120: *What's Missing?*

1. 6
2. 2
3. 0
4. 4
5. 7
6. 9
7. 5
8. 8
9. 6
10. 5
11. 3
12. 4
13. 9
14. 8
15. 2
16. 3
17. 3
18. 9
19. 4
20. 4

Page 121: *Which Is Bigger?*

1. ▶
2. =
3. ◀
4. ◀
5. =
6. =
7. ◀
8. ▶
9. ▶
10. ◀
11. ▶
12. =

Page 122: *Order, Please!*

1. 13 – 9
   15 – 9
   8 – 0
   13 – 4

2. 10 – 6
   12 – 6
   15 – 7
   14 – 5

3. 7 – 6
   5 – 3
   10 – 4
   11 – 4

4. 8 – 4
   8 – 3
   11 – 5
   11 – 4

5. 8 – 7
   5 – 1
   6 – 0
   9 – 0

6. 11 – 5
   16 – 9
   13 – 5
   14 – 5

7. 9 – 5
   14 – 9
   15 – 9
   16 – 7

8. 12 – 9
   6 – 0
   15 – 8
   10 – 2

Page 123: *Find All the Smallies*

1. 2
2. 1
3. 7
4. 7
5. 1
6. 5
7. 4
8. 5
9. 3
10. 4
11. 3
12. 2

The secret words are: MATH SMALLIES

Page 124: *Who Are the Twins?*

1, 2, 4, 5, 7, 8, 11, 12, 13, 14

Page 125: *The Right Location*

1.	9 – 8	**2.**	11 – 9	**3.**	7 – 4
	6 – 5		9 – 7		10 – 7
	8 – 7		8 – 6		11 – 8

4.	9 – 5	**5.**	13 – 8	**6.**	13 – 7
	10 – 6		14 – 9		12 – 6
	12 – 8		9 – 4		14 – 8

7.	12 – 5	**8.**	12 – 4	**9.**	14 – 5
	14 – 7		10 – 2		11 – 2
	15 – 8		16 – 8		13 – 4

Page 126: *Odds and Evens*

The odd items are:

12 – 7   13 – 4   5 – 2   12 – 3   15 – 8
11 – 8   13 – 6   10 – 7   8 – 3   9 – 2

The even answers are items numbered:
3, 5, 8, 13, 14, 18, 19

When an even number is subtracted from an even number, you get an even difference.

When an odd number is subtracted from an odd number, you get an even difference.

Page 130: *Match Me!*

1: 3, 0, 9, 8
2: 8, 5, 7, 3
3: 4, 2, 6, 3
4: 5, 6, 9, 8

Page 132: *Find Left-out Louie*

1. 8		**2.** 6		**3.** 1	
4. 0		**5.** 5		**6.** 8	
7. 3		**8.** 9		**9.** 9	
10. 6		**11.** 5		**12.** 9	
13. 7		**14.** 1		**15.** 7	
16. 4		**17.** 1		**18.** 3	
19. 8		**20.** 4		**21.** 2	
22. 4		**23.** 2		**24.** 0	

Left-out Louie: 2

Page 133: *Subtraction One-Minute Challenge #1*

	a	b	c	d	e	f
1.	1	0	1	5	2	9
2.	6	5	7	9	6	0
3.	8	0	7	9	6	3
4.	3	9	7	8	4	5
5.	0	8	0	5	5	7

Page 134: *Subtraction One-Minute Challenge #2*

	a	b	c	d	e	f
1.	4	7	4	3	7	9
2.	8	2	0	0	6	9
3.	1	5	5	7	6	6
4.	9	2	5	6	9	9
5.	7	0	7	3	0	9

Page 135: *Subtraction One-Minute Challenge #3*

	a	b	c	d	e	f
1.	2	4	7	9	5	1
2.	5	5	2	6	6	5
3.	4	4	4	8	6	8
4.	8	1	8	3	3	9
5.	9	7	1	9	7	6

Page 136: *Subtraction One-Minute Challenge #4*

	a	b	c	d	e	f
1.	5	2	3	7	0	7
2.	7	2	6	2	8	8
3.	6	4	0	8	6	8
4.	3	4	8	3	9	2
5.	9	3	3	6	7	7

Page 137: *Subtraction One-Minute Challenge #5*

	a	b	c	d	e	f
1.	4	0	4	5	7	5
2.	4	2	3	9	7	6
3.	4	5	6	8	6	7
4.	7	1	6	6	2	8
5.	5	4	5	4	5	6

Page 139: *Subtraction Practice Test #1*

	a	b	c	d	e	f	g	h	i	j
1.	5	6	2	7	9	3	4	0	8	1
2.	1	5	3	2	8	7	0	9	6	4
3.	7	2	4	0	5	9	6	1	3	8
4.	2	8	0	4	7	0	9	6	5	3
5.	3	2	1	5	0	9	4	7	6	8
6.	3	4	6	1	7	5	9	0	2	8
7.	9	8	3	1	0	7	2	5	6	4
8.	3	0	2	1	4	7	9	2	6	8
9.	1	8	7	4	2	5	6	3	9	1
10.	8	4	7	1	5	0	5	3	9	6

Page 140: *Subtraction Practice Test #2*

	a	b	c	d	e
1.	3	3	9	8	4
2.	7	9	0	5	3
3.	5	1	3	3	0
4.	8	0	3	8	8
5.	2	1	0	7	4
6.	6	6	9	1	4
7.	4	2	4	8	4
8.	7	8	8	3	5
9.	1	6	2	2	0
10.	3	5	2	9	2
11.	6	7	9	1	4
12.	3	5	6	7	8
13.	9	9	2	2	0
14.	5	1	6	1	0
15.	6	5	1	1	9
16.	4	0	7	7	5
17.	8	0	6	2	5
18.	9	6	5	7	3
19.	7	4	9	6	8
20.	7	1	0	2	4

Page 141: *Subtraction Practice Test #3*

	a	b	c	d	e	f	g	h	i	j
1.	4	2	9	6	7	2	9	5	2	9
2.	5	7	6	5	7	5	4	7	5	5
3.	2	4	6	2	6	5	0	2	6	8
4.	1	4	2	8	6	4	5	8	4	5
5.	8	6	8	6	0	4	1	6	8	3
6.	1	0	4	4	8	8	3	4	0	9
7.	7	1	0	9	0	1	0	3	1	0
8.	8	3	9	0	3	1	7	3	8	2
9.	5	9	1	3	2	9	1	7	1	9
10.	7	3	2	3	7	9	0	3	7	6

Page 142: *Subtraction Practice Test #4*

	a	b	c	d	e	f	g	h	i	j
1.	3	7	7	3	4	5	3	6	9	2
2.	1	3	9	5	9	1	9	1	7	2
3.	3	1	8	7	3	2	8	0	3	9
4.	1	0	1	7	0	3	1	9	4	0
5.	0	0	4	8	4	0	2	9	3	8
6.	6	8	3	4	8	6	6	8	0	1
7.	1	8	2	7	5	4	5	8	4	6
8.	2	6	4	2	6	5	1	2	6	8
9.	0	0	4	9	7	7	5	5	5	7
10.	4	5	6	2	9	5	2	9	7	6

Page 143: *Subtraction Practice Test #5*

	a	b	c	d	e	f	g	h	i	j
1.	1	9	3	0	9	4	8	0	8	0
2.	2	5	7	9	6	8	3	4	9	9
3.	1	2	7	1	9	0	8	3	7	8
4.	5	2	4	6	4	0	7	5	5	8
5.	1	6	2	4	6	3	9	6	7	8
6.	8	4	3	3	3	0	3	4	7	5
7.	5	8	1	7	2	2	0	5	1	7
8.	6	6	2	0	5	4	7	9	4	4
9.	3	9	1	9	0	7	2	1	1	8
10.	1	3	6	2	6	6	2	5	0	5

Page 144: *Subtraction Diagnostic Test*

	a	b	c	d	e	f	g	h	i	j
1.	4	0	9	6	7	2	9	5	2	9
2.	4	1	5	3	6	9	4	7	0	8
3.	5	8	2	3	4	1	8	0	6	6
4.	2	1	7	3	8	9	7	5	2	2
5.	4	1	0	5	1	6	3	8	1	6
6.	3	0	0	4	9	6	9	3	9	7
7.	7	7	2	6	5	8	1	6	0	3
8.	1	8	8	7	3	0	3	5	1	4
9.	0	4	5	1	4	3	8	9	5	7
10.	6	2	2	9	7	2	0	8	5	4

Ten-Ten Frame

Ten Frame

Flash Card Template for Addition and Subtraction Facts

Directions: Make multiple copies. On each card, write a number fact. Use for both addition and subtraction. For durability, paste the cards to tagboard or index cards. To make addition cards, change – to **+** .

Triangular Flash Cards Template

Directions: Copy this template and paste it onto tagboard. Then cut out the four triangles on each duplicated sheet. On the front of each card, write a number fact with the combination numbers in the bottom corners. On the back, do the same and write the sum in the apex.

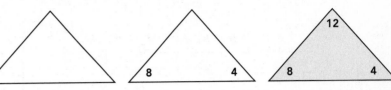

Addition-Subtraction Tables

Directions: Copy and cut apart these Addition-Subtraction Tables so that all students have their own. Suggest that students tape the table to their desk or folder to use as a reference tool. Model how the table serves both addition and subtraction needs.

+	0	1	2	3	4	5	6	7	8	9
0	0	1	2	3	4	5	6	7	8	9
1	1	2	3	4	5	6	7	8	9	10
2	2	3	4	5	6	7	8	9	10	11
3	3	4	5	6	7	8	9	10	11	12
4	4	5	6	7	8	9	10	11	12	13
5	5	6	7	8	9	10	11	12	13	14
6	6	7	8	9	10	11	12	13	14	15
7	7	8	9	10	11	12	13	14	15	16
8	8	9	10	11	12	13	14	15	16	17
9	9	10	11	12	13	14	15	16	17	18

+	0	1	2	3	4	5	6	7	8	9
0	0	1	2	3	4	5	6	7	8	9
1	1	2	3	4	5	6	7	8	9	10
2	2	3	4	5	6	7	8	9	10	11
3	3	4	5	6	7	8	9	10	11	12
4	4	5	6	7	8	9	10	11	12	13
5	5	6	7	8	9	10	11	12	13	14
6	6	7	8	9	10	11	12	13	14	15
7	7	8	9	10	11	12	13	14	15	16
8	8	9	10	11	12	13	14	15	16	17
9	9	10	11	12	13	14	15	16	17	18

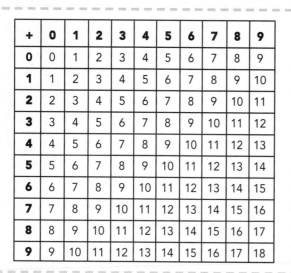

+	0	1	2	3	4	5	6	7	8	9
0	0	1	2	3	4	5	6	7	8	9
1	1	2	3	4	5	6	7	8	9	10
2	2	3	4	5	6	7	8	9	10	11
3	3	4	5	6	7	8	9	10	11	12
4	4	5	6	7	8	9	10	11	12	13
5	5	6	7	8	9	10	11	12	13	14
6	6	7	8	9	10	11	12	13	14	15
7	7	8	9	10	11	12	13	14	15	16
8	8	9	10	11	12	13	14	15	16	17
9	9	10	11	12	13	14	15	16	17	18

+	0	1	2	3	4	5	6	7	8	9
0	0	1	2	3	4	5	6	7	8	9
1	1	2	3	4	5	6	7	8	9	10
2	2	3	4	5	6	7	8	9	10	11
3	3	4	5	6	7	8	9	10	11	12
4	4	5	6	7	8	9	10	11	12	13
5	5	6	7	8	9	10	11	12	13	14
6	6	7	8	9	10	11	12	13	14	15
7	7	8	9	10	11	12	13	14	15	16
8	8	9	10	11	12	13	14	15	16	17
9	9	10	11	12	13	14	15	16	17	18

+	0	1	2	3	4	5	6	7	8	9
0	0	1	2	3	4	5	6	7	8	9
1	1	2	3	4	5	6	7	8	9	10
2	2	3	4	5	6	7	8	9	10	11
3	3	4	5	6	7	8	9	10	11	12
4	4	5	6	7	8	9	10	11	12	13
5	5	6	7	8	9	10	11	12	13	14
6	6	7	8	9	10	11	12	13	14	15
7	7	8	9	10	11	12	13	14	15	16
8	8	9	10	11	12	13	14	15	16	17
9	9	10	11	12	13	14	15	16	17	18

+	0	1	2	3	4	5	6	7	8	9
0	0	1	2	3	4	5	6	7	8	9
1	1	2	3	4	5	6	7	8	9	10
2	2	3	4	5	6	7	8	9	10	11
3	3	4	5	6	7	8	9	10	11	12
4	4	5	6	7	8	9	10	11	12	13
5	5	6	7	8	9	10	11	12	13	14
6	6	7	8	9	10	11	12	13	14	15
7	7	8	9	10	11	12	13	14	15	16
8	8	9	10	11	12	13	14	15	16	17
9	9	10	11	12	13	14	15	16	17	18

Addition and Subtraction B-I-N-G-O

Directions: Duplicate for both addition and subtraction practice. See directions on page 71.

B	I	N	G	O
		Free		

Student Response Cards

Directions: Copy and distribute these cards so that each student has a set. Have students cut out their set. During fact-review activities have students give answers by raising the card with the answer. (If you say: *0+1*, then students should show the card with 1 on it.) Explain to students that if the answer is 10 or more, they should use two cards together. You'll find an extra 1 card so that students can make 11.

7

4

1

8

5

2

0

9

6

3

1